T0328276

CULTURAL

STUDIES

Volume 3   Number 2   May 1989

Special Issue:

EUROPEAN IDENTITIES

CULTURAL STUDIES is a new international journal, dedicated to the notion that the study of cultural processes, and especially of popular culture, is important, complex, and both theoretically and politically rewarding. It is published three times a year, with issues being edited in rotation from Australia, the UK and the USA, though occasional issues will be edited from elsewhere. Its international editorial collective consists of scholars representing the range of the most influential disciplinary and theoretical approaches to cultural studies.

CULTURAL STUDIES will be in the vanguard of developments in the area worldwide, putting academics, researchers, students and practitioners in different countries and from diverse intellectual traditions in touch with each other and each other's work. Its lively international dialogue will take the form not only of scholarly research and discourse, but also of new forms of writing, photo essays, cultural reviews and political interventions.

CULTURAL STUDIES will publish articles on those practices, texts and cultural domains within which the various social groups that constitute a late capitalist society negotiate patterns of power and meaning. It will engage with the interplay between the personal and the political, between strategies of domination and resistance, between meaning systems and social systems.

CULTURAL STUDIES will seek to develop and transform those perspectives which have traditionally informed the field — structuralism and semiotics, Marxism, psychoanalysis and feminism. Theories of discourse, of power, of pleasure and of the institutionalization of meaning are crucial to its enterprise; so too are those which stress the ethnography of culture.

Contributions should be sent to either the General Editor or one of the Associate Editors. They should be in duplicate and should conform to the reference system set out in the Notes for Contributors, available from the Editors or Publishers. They make take the form of articles of about 5000 words, of kites (short, provocative or exploratory pieces) of about 2000 words, or of reviews of books, other cultural texts or events.

EUROPEAN IDENTITIES

CURRENT SOCIOLOGY
La sociologie contemporaine
A Journal of the International Sociological Association

Edited by **William Outhwaite** *University of Sussex*

Each issue of this unique journal is devoted to a comprehensive Trend Report on a topic of interest to the international community of sociologists. Authors review current trends and tendencies in all areas of sociological work — theories, methods, concepts, substantive research and national or regional developments. The aim is to review new developments, to discuss controversies, and to provide extensive bibliographies. From time to time, Commentaries on Trend Reports are published in subsequent issues of the journal.

Recent reports have focused on the multinational version of social science, different traditions of sociology and the human body, the sociology of law, migration in Europe, the sociology of industrial and post-industrial societies, and the sociology of humour and laughter.

Issues are published in French or English, but a text in one language is always accompanied by an extensive resume in the other. **Current Sociology** is an official journal of the International Sociological Association. Its main aim is to review international developments in the discipline and to provide a forum from which professional sociologists from all countries can communicate with the widest group of colleagues.

Current Sociology is published three times a year in Spring, Summer and Winter
ISSN: 0011-3921

Subscription Rates, 1988

	Institutional	Individual
one year	£50.00($75.00)	£22.00($33.00)
two years	£99.00($148.50)	£44.00($66.00)
single copies	£17.00($25.50)	£8.00($12.00)

SAGE Publications Ltd, 28 Banner Street, London EC1Y 8QE
SAGE Publications Ltd, PO Box 5096, Newbury Park, CA 91359

· INTRODUCTION ·

IEN ANG AND DAVID MORLEY

MAYONNAISE CULTURE AND OTHER EUROPEAN FOLLIES

Putting together a 'European Issue' for this journal proved to be a very intriguing task – not least because of the complexity of what 'Europe' means. Europe is not just a geographical site, it is also an idea: an idea inextricably linked with the myths of western civilization, and its implications not only of culture but also of colonialism. Twentieth-century Europe is also a political and historical reality that continues to be marked by the deeply traumatic experiences of World War II and the drawing of the Iron Curtain – a continent whose century-long world hegemony was gradually taken over by the United States on the one side, and the Soviet Union on the other.

This marginalization of Europe's place in the developed world is still felt as painful and unjustified in important centres of the European power-bloc – a sentiment which has contributed considerably to the postwar re-emergence of a movement towards European unification, as a remedy for Europe's weakened position. Of course, Europe has never been a political, economic, and cultural unity, but the *idea* of, and indeed desire for, a European unity has always played a (contradictory) role in European politics. In recent years, this idea has gained renewed momentum, with the coming economic and administrative integration of the EEC (European Economic Community) countries in 1992. And with the advent of the age of satellite broadcasting, the old relationships between national culture and political sovereignty are already being undone by the creation of transnational 'communities' of the airwaves. As Rath has put it, 'frontiers of a national, regional or cultural kind no longer count; what counts much more is the boundary of the territory of transmission' (Rath, 1985: 202) – which increasingly bears little relationship to the geographical territory of any given nation-state. As the transnationals of the airwaves move into operation, it is increasingly difficult for any national government to 'endow a culture with its own political roof' (Gellner, 1983: 43). In this situation, the historically established couplings of polity and culture, which have created the nations of Europe as we know them, appear increasingly tenuous.

However, all the macro-talk of unification and integration – whether euphoric or apocalyptic – tends to obscure the fact that inside and between the particular European nations a myriad of heterogeneous political and cultural struggles are being fought out, along the axes of class, gender, and ethnicity, as well as around language, religion, and regionality – all struggles which tend to fracture the image of unity preferred by the administrative elite and endorsed by the transnational, corporate world. In this 'European issue', then, we would like to stress the tensions between unity and diversity, forces of unification and forces of diversification, which in our view characterize life in Europe in the late 1980s.

A 'European issue' of this journal could also be expected to represent work stemming from notional 'European Cultural Studies'. However, there is no such thing. As Europe is by no means a unity, it would be absurd to expect a homogeneous intellectual climate on the continent as a whole – in that sense, the use of the term 'European', as such, runs the danger of mystifying rather than clarifying intellectual, cultural, and political realities and relations. In this issue articles have been written by authors both from countries located in the north-west of the continent (countries where English is a common second language), and from Britain – reflecting the biases of the two editors.

As a nation, Britain has always been very ambivalent about its place in Europe, defining itself as both inside and outside of it. This ambivalence has profound roots in British political culture and has been manifested, in recent years, in both Right (e.g. Enoch Powell) and Left (e.g. Tony Benn) forms of 'Little Englandism' – a form of cultural politics which, as Gilroy (1986) has noted, is ultimately based in racist categories. Over the last few years we have also been treated to the spectacle of English football fans terrorizing European cities (Heysel Stadium, Belgium, 1985; European Championships, West Germany, 1988), in the latter case proudly wearing their 'British Tour of Europe 1939–45/1988' T-shirts, while singing Fascist songs.[1] Even more recently, we have witnessed the contradictory sight of the heir to the British throne enthusing about the benefits of European unification, while the British Prime Minister backs herself into a corner, from which she defends the narrowest forms of nationalism, against the threat posed to British sovereignty by Brussels.

Against this background of British isolationism, it is ironic that while cultural studies in its contemporary form was more or less a British invention, it has become such a highly exportable item. Cultural studies can now be considered an international phenomenon – this very journal is testimony to that. It is the internationalization of cultural studies that we wish to address here, before going into what, in our view, are some of the important issues to be dealt with by cultural studies in relation to recent European developments.

Cultural studies as an export industry

As an intellectual enterprise, cultural studies has, in key ways, depended for its development and orientation on a particular sensibility to its own social and political contexts. In Britain, cultural studies has been a major driving force in post-1968 leftwing intellectual culture. Its political allegiances have been explicit and direct – not least, in the last decade or so, when the British Left has been faced with the tenacious hegemony of Thatcherism. In this situation, cultural studies has served as one site on which Left intellectual opposition to Thatcherite discourse has been developed and organized. The theoretical heritage which began with the work of Richard Hoggart and Raymond Williams and which flourished in the 1970s at the Birmingham Centre for Contemporary Cultural Studies, can still be found operative in, for instance, critical magazines such as *Marxism Today* and *New Socialist*, enabling an ongoing theoretical engagement with cultural issues. Cultural studies in Britain may, against this background, be described as an intellectual *movement* whose theoretical and political impact has at various points reached beyond the walls of the university, even if it is currently in a period of institutional retrenchment within British academia.

However, British cultural studies has also become a model for 'progressive' students and academics in other countries, who have sought for inspiration in their attempts to develop alternative intellectual practices. However this does not mean that cultural studies is a fixed body of thought, that can be transported from one place to another, and which operates in similar ways in diverse national or regional contexts. Thus, the recent boom of cultural studies in the United States, for example, has generally been a purely academic matter. Indeed, as Stuart Hall (1986) has observed, 'in America, cultural studies is sometimes used as just one more paradigm.'

In American cultural studies, then, theoretical sophistication often seems to override any sense of concrete political engagement and involvement. Perhaps because of the marginalized position in which the American Left finds itself, it is in the United States that the Althusserian idea of theoretical practice – as a political activity in its own right – has found its most zealous proponents, at a time when the Althusserian project seems only a dim memory for the European intellectual Left. Furthermore, it is perhaps because of the highly abstracted form of intellectual development of cultural studies in America that postmodernism has become such a central object of analysis in American cultural studies – if, that is, the postmodern is diagnosed, as Lawrence Grossberg (1988a: 290) puts it, as 'a crisis of the very possibility of politics.' That cultural studies, as an intellectual practice, remains a problematic activity in American academia is indicated by the critical (not to say hostile) responses some of its more theoretically inclined (if not theoreticist) proponents have attracted from American scholars with a commitment to a more empirically grounded approach (cf. Lull, 1988).

However, the export of British cultural studies has not been confined to the United States. It has also been transplanted elsewhere, and the sites of these transplantations (Australia, Canada) have often ironically echoed the original map of British imperialism's conquests. Thus, we find a recent correspondent in *Screen* puzzling over 'strange-new-world factors' such as the 'inordinate number of left academics wandering round Australia, but talking about Birmingham' (Francovits, 1987: 122).

As an international phenomenon, then, cultural studies is, at the same time, a movement, a paradigm and an intellectual fad. It remains largely restricted to the developed world, reflecting the fact that it is in the west that the cultural dimension of politics has been foregrounded, as a result of transformations in the social formation brought about by post-industrial and post-Fordist capitalism (Hall, 1988). It is also, for that matter, pretty much an Anglo-American affair.[2] In Italy, for instance, a formal institutionalization of something called cultural studies would seem to be both academically and politically nonsensical, because ongoing politically motivated cultural analysis has long been an integrated part of Italy's general intellectual culture – which, to a certain extent, overflows into the pages of the daily newspapers and the image flows of the television screen (see *Cultural Studies'* Italian issue, May 1988).

In other words, the place and relevance of cultural studies varies from context to context, and has to be related to the specific character of local forms of political and intellectual discourse on culture. In our view, it is the context-dependence of cultural studies which we need to keep in mind, and indeed reinforce, if we are to resist tendencies towards the development of orthodoxies and the temptations of a codified vocabulary – tendencies which may be the less desirable effect of internationalization. And this brings us to the situation in north-west Europe.

One thing is evident: countries like Holland, West Germany, Denmark, Norway, and Sweden do not have a clearly discernible cultural studies scene. Academic work that could be considered to be within the category of cultural studies is being undertaken here and there, but is scattered all over the place, and it is certainly not part of a collective intellectual movement. Furthermore, what is sadly missing in north-west European public discourse is any sustained, Left intellectual interest in discussing matters of contemporary culture in a critical yet openminded way. Gabriele Kreutzner argues in this issue that, in West Germany, this lack is related to the continuing hegemony within the Left of Frankfurt School Critical Theory. But there may also be other reasons why there should be such an indifference, if not incompetence, among west European Left intellectuals towards developing an independent critical discourse on the relation of politics and culture.

Perhaps one of the most important disabling circumstances, in this respect, is the dominance, in spirit if not in practice, of a social democratic vision of culture in postwar western Europe. For social democracy, with its concept of the welfare state, to be built up through rational institutional reform and planning, cultural politics becomes a matter of cultural policy: a set of state-directed practices, guided by pedagogical aims presented as democracy, in which 'politics tend to be treated as a specialist, expert realm into which the rude noises of "the population" rarely intrude, or, if they do, they do so mainly as "constraints" on policy makers' (CCCS, 1981: 13–14).

This conception is notably manifested in policies for cultural education and distribution, in which culture (generally still defined in high-cultural terms) is seen as a fixed value that needs to be disseminated throughout the whole population. As a result, the role assigned to 'the people' is exclusively that of receivers, not of producers of culture – an assumption fundamentally at odds with the perspective developed within British cultural studies. It is not for nothing, for example, that in the Netherlands the work of what has tenaciously been called the Birmingham 'school' has been most influential in departments of education, where Paul Willis's (1977) study of antischool culture has found more resonance than, for instance, Dick Hebdige's (1979) less institutionally-focused emphasis on the politics of style. This can be explained by the fact that, from a generalized social democratic perspective, interest in forms of cultural resistance is cast in the desire to (better) *teach* 'the people', not to *learn* from popular experiences. In such a context, anything other than an 'administrative' notion of cultural politics is hardly conceivable, while popular cultural practices develop without being taken seriously by the intellectual Left.

'Postmodernism is for older people'

Meanwhile, the European cultural landscape of the 1980s is, as has been noted earlier, increasingly confusing and, from the perspective of the cultural policy makers, increasingly unmanageable. Greater fragmentation and pluralism, the weakening of older collective solidarities and identities, the increasing dependence of cultural production on market forces, and, at the same time, an increasing tendency among urban youths to develop their own cultural agendas – all this might ring the familiar bell of post-modernism.

However, perhaps not so surprisingly, while postmodernism has enjoyed an intellectual vogue in most European countries in recent years, the concept has not necessarily led to any sustained assessment of concrete cultural developments. 'Pomo' has, at most, become an (overused and meaningless) journalistic term to designate anything hip, fancy, and fashionable. Some young people even self-consciously consider themselves as beyond post-modernism. Thus, one young local media activist from Amsterdam who calls himself an 'illegal intellectual' says, shrugging his shoulders, 'Post-modernism is for older people, for people who are still struggling with their pasts. We don't have that problem. We are sovereign.' Consciously living from social welfare (a strategic option opened up within the very interstices of social democratic social policy), former members of the Amsterdam squatters' movement (which, as a political movement, had its heyday in the early 1980s) have developed their own social and cultural infrastructure – media (pirate radio, magazines), shops, bars – which they don't want to call 'alternative' or 'oppositional', but 'sovereign'. This kind of 'sovereign' cultural politics, however, remains largely subterranean and more often than not goes unrecognized among the established Left.

While recognizing the importance of the insights of many theorists working within the paradigm(s) of 'postmodernism', we would want to argue that the perspectives they offer too often remain at too generalized and abstract a level of analysis to be directly helpful in understanding developments such as those sketched above. It may also be important to locate postmodernism itself, as an intellectual movement, within its own socio-historical context. Thus, Paul Gilroy has suggested that postmodernism can also usefully be understood as a symptom of the 'crisis' of the downwardly mobile white intellectuals of western Europe, working in a decaying public sector.[3] All in all, postmodern theory offers too easily the possibility of projecting an *a priori* theoretical schema onto the heterogeneous and specific complexities of the cultural conjuncture in which we find ourselves. Thus, as Meaghan Morris (1987) remarked in her review of Baudrillard's *Amérique*, it is all too possible for the most sophisticated theorist to visit a place (and certainly if the theorist is European and the place is America) and find nothing but ready-made, confirming 'instances' of the General Theory – which has already been pre-constructed, needing only a ground on which to stand. Morris notes that amongst other things, 'Baudrillard's itinerary depends on an assiduous avoidance of conversation with flesh and blood Americans'.

In response, what we appeal for here is not some easy form of flat empiricism. It goes without saying that encounters with flesh and blood Americans alone would not suffice for a culturally sensitive understanding of 'America' either. Recently, it has been argued that ethnographic work is centrally flawed by the way in which it constructs its subjects as 'Others', at the receiving end of the attentions of the distanced analyst. Against this ethnographic perspective, Lawrence Grossberg has argued that we are all, in fact, 'nomadic subjects', and to that extent, as analysts, we too inhabit, in our everyday lives, the spaces of mass-mediated popular culture, no differently in principle, from other people. Thus, he asserts that 'within the domain of contemporary cultural practices the Other is never any more exotic or strange than we are. In so far as Otherness is effective in the field of media culture, the nomadic subject is always other to itself' (1988b: 388). While he is right to warn against the dangers of *a priori* assessments of pertinent differences between ourselves and others, it is in our view a particularly depoliticizing move to conclude that 'everybody' is the same – mirroring the image of the postmodern 'nomadic subject' conjured up by the theorist! We may all be 'nomadic' in some fundamental sense, constantly moving between different subject positions, but we visit very different locations on our journeys, and some of us are travelling by plane, some by bike, and some by foot – or, like Baudrillard, 'asleep at the wheel' in Morris' deathless phrase – and these material differences are regretfully suppressed by the emphasis on the sense in which we are all, at an abstract level, nomadic. This is also a very individualizing perspective – which obscures the sense in which our individualities are still framed within the structures of class, gender, race, religion, region, and politics, to name but a few of the more obvious factors. It is one thing to say, as Barthes does, that the true critic of popular culture must also possess the capacity to be a fan, and to that extent partakes of the ordinary world as others do. It is quite another to imply, as Grossberg seems to do, that our participation in the ordinary world can somehow guarantee us against what Paul Willis (1980) has called the 'surprises' of ethnographic encounters with others.

Some of the articles collected here are dependent emphatically on 'conversation' with flesh and blood Europeans. And although such an ethnographic approach should not be celebrated as the only 'correct' mode of analysis, concern with the historically and culturally specific remains, for us, at a theoretical level, a pre-eminent guiding principle. In commissioning articles for this issue, then, we have worked from the premise that the current cultural situation in western Europe needs to be assessed through more specific concerns and concrete vantage points than the generalized ones of postmodernism.

Some concrete 'posts'

Kevin Robins offers an important analysis of some current transformations in European image markets. According to Robins, these transformations should not simply be interpreted in the technologically determinist terms of a new 'communications revolution' or the coming of an 'information society'. Rather, what is at stake is a fundamental transformation in geographic relationships: a new politics of space and place, and a new dialectic of concurrent pressures – both towards 'globalization' and, at the same time, towards 'localization'. These large-scale, structural tendencies will have far-reaching consequences for the ways in which culture is created and consumed.

Changing patterns of cultural consumption in postwar Europe have been accompanied by some persistent ideological themes which, contrary to what is often claimed, are far from being eradicated by the discourse of postmodernism. For instance, the perceived threat of the 'Americanization' of European culture has been a key theme in cultural debates concerning European identities since the late nineteenth century. The postwar period has seen a particularly marked resurgence of these fears, perhaps expressed most strongly by Jack Lang during his period as French Minister of Culture. Thus, at a conference in Mexico, in 1982, Lang explained that, in his view, Europe's 'cultural and artistic creation . . . is today victim of a system of multinational financial domination against which we must organise ourselves. . . . Is it our destiny to become the vassals of an immense empire of profit?', he asked, going on to call for 'genuine cultural resistance against this domination . . . this financial and intellectual imperialism.' (Quoted in Mattelart et al., 1984, p. 14.)

It is *against* some image of 'America' or, as Duncan Webster (1988) has put it elsewhere, 'the imaginary America of populist culture' (usually equated with trivialization, the destruction of traditional standards, and the threat of 'Coca Cola culture') that European identities have often been defined. 'America' has provided the image of what 'we' are not; or that which 'we' do not wish to imagine ourselves to be; or that which it is feared 'we' are about to become.

However, the terms of the postwar cultural settlement between Europe and America have always been contradictory. In many European nations (including the Soviet Union) American popular culture has often played a complex role, not least in attracting the allegiance of working-class audiences for whom the 'vulgar' products of the American culture industry have often provided more amenable points of identification than the (class-ridden) forms of their own national cultures (cf. Hebdige, 1988). If Hollywood ever colonized the subconscious of postwar Europe then it was with the knowing complicity of large numbers of Europeans. Indeed, as Simon Frith has put it elsewhere, in this process 'America', as experienced in films and music, has itself become the prime object of consumption, a symbol of pleasure. But Frith also points to the rise of 'Europop' as an independent set of musical sensibilities.

And now, while the European nations still wrangle over their respective attempts to protect their cultural sovereignty from this 'American invasion', the terms are shifting yet again. As the United States begins to face the consequences of having become the world's largest debtor nation, and as the pivot of the world economy swings from the Atlantic to the Pacific basin, a fundamental modification in the balance of economic power is taking place, whose impacts have begun to make themselves felt in the cultural sphere as well. Sony's purchase of CBS presages what may yet turn out to be a fundamental realignment of international cultural forces, and the old cultural ramparts along Europe's Atlantic coast may well turn out to be facing in quite the wrong direction. In fact, European nations may now face the prospect of a different form of marginalization from the world stage, a prospect that throws the threat of 'Americanization' into quite a new perspective.

The theme of 'Americanization' is discussed here by Duncan Webster in his analysis of the significance of 'Rambo' in recent British debates over crime, television, and cultural discipline. The fear of 'Americanization' is closely related to another theme: the continuing preoccupation with the dichotomy between 'high' and 'low' culture on the European continent – a dichotomy which is so deeply entrenched in official cultural policies that, ironically enough, when pop musicians in Holland articulate their claim for state subsidy, they do so through a discourse of Art. The two themes ('Americanization' and 'high/low culture') have in common that they provide a *moral evaluative* discourse on culture, that is, a discourse which functions to regulate the validation of cultural objects and practices.

Thus, the increasing commercialization of Amsterdam's main square, Leidseplein, traditionally a centre of approved forms of high and middle-brow culture (theatres, art cinemas, 'non-commercial' rock, and popular music, as well as classical architecture) has recently been lamented by a group of concerned citizens, who have disgustedly dubbed this process of what this incident signifies for me is the insight into the necessity of a *Streitkultur* (a culture of controversy) informed by the widest possible range of differing voices which I have come to see as a prerequisite for the development of critical thinking about culture and society. And while a *Streitkultur* does not necessarily manifest itself as the kind of cosy and harmonious enterprise evoked by my little anecdote, I think that such a context is essential for the emergence of a productive as well as pleasurable critical discourse.

It is such a *Streitkultur* about cultural phenomena that I miss in West German academic and intellectual life. And while the 'discovery' of a variety of recent critical work on contemporary culture done in Australia, Great Britain, and the United States has contributed in no small way to my political motivation and my pleasure in cultural studies, in West Germany there does not seem to be any widely shared conviction that to study contemporary culture in its heterogeneity and diversity is politically and theoretically significant and that critical thinking can and should be something pleasurable.

This is not to say, however, that there is no such thing as cultural studies in this country. Indeed, one can trace a range of spaces in West German academic and intellectual life today where cultural studies (in the sense of the approach developed by the British Centre for Contemporary Cultural Studies) have emerged. As in Great Britain, the 1970s saw the development of the history workshop movement; lately, *Alltagsgeschichte* (everyday life history) has made its contributions to the field. Furthermore, the Argument Verlag in West Berlin provides an outlet for projects which can be subsumed under the label of cultural studies. As its editorial committee puts it, the publishing house is dedicated to 'a theoretical culture of the Left'. Of particular interest to me are various projects that developed around the 'critical psychology' group. For example, a number of feminist projects studying everyday life history in terms of the constitution of the gendered subject has been published since 1980 (Haug, 1984; Haug and Hauser, 1985, 1986). These publications present the collective practices by women in Hamburg and West Berlin of writing and analysing their own autobiographical accounts, and thereby seeking to understand and change their positions within patriarchal ideology. Recently, the 'critical psychology' group has done research on *Ausländerfeindlichkeit*, investigating specific forms of xenophobia and racism in West Germany. While this work is yet to be published, a project of this type is of particular importance in the context context of the current tightening of the terms under which western European countries are prepared to offer political asylum to refugees from countries such as the Lebanon, Iran and Chile. The 'critical psychology' group not only analyses the broad functions of racism in the current climate of economic recession and political (neo-)conservatism, but also in a more concrete sense is concerned with the specifically bureaucratic forms of racism experienced by these refugees.

In a more restricted sense, the work of the Ludwig-Uhland-Institut für empirische Kulturwissenschaft (LUI) in Tübingen has to be seen as the eating habits or our television diet. Thus, in Britain, the constitution of the new Broadcasting Standards Council, under the chairmanship of the ex-head of the Arts Council, William Rees-Mogg, returns the question of 'standards' to a quite central place in the debates surrounding the future of broadcasting. 'Standards', in this context, denotes a far wider set of concerns than any narrow squabble about the explicit forms of 'political bias'. Rather, a far wider field of cultural products is now to be subject to a new form of cultural policing, under the guise of the respectably 'a-political' concern with protecting public 'standards' of taste and decency.

It is interesting to note, however, that this puritan obsession with 'standards' is a particularly British phenomenon. In countries like Holland, Germany, France, and Italy, the advent of commercial broadcast television has, among other things, led to the relatively uncontested expansion of programmes and shows with titles such as *The Pin Up Club* and *Supersexy*, containing soft porn and other forms of 'eroticism', taking commercial television further along this road than it has travelled even in America.

Against this background, it may not only be the Right which needs recourse to notions of 'standards', even if the terms within which the issue might be addressed by the Left would need to be formulated differently – for example, in terms of sexual politics rather than through the high-cultural discourse of debasement and falling moral standards. What the practical resilience of the 'high/low' dichotomy in European cultural politics suggests, is the necessity for progressive forces not to discard concern over 'standards' altogether, but rather to find alternative discourses of evaluation. Thus, according to Jostein Gripsrud, it is important, both theoretically and politically, to retain some notion of 'distinction' – not least because it can function as a healthy self-reflexive device for cultural studies scholars themselves. It is interesting, in this connection, that Gripsrud's attempt to rework this currently unfashionable approach to the analysis of culture is but a part of a wider tendency in European intellectual perspectives. Thus Gripsrud's work should be seen in the context both of other recent Scandinavian work on the question of cultural quality (cf. Schröder, 1988) and in relation to Charlotte Brunsdon's (1989) attempt to put the question 'What is good television?' back on the agenda of cultural studies.

Meanwhile, the new technologies are rapidly changing the parameters of everyday culture, in Europe as well as in other parts of the world. The Marxist 'grand narrative' of the new technologies is well-known: in that story they are the carriers of an ever more large-scale, world-wide mono-culture. However, as we have already noted in relation to Kevin Robins' contribution to this issue, equally important is the dialectic of the local and the global: new communities and identities are constantly being built and rebuilt, in a world which seems to be increasingly dominated by a global cultural repertoire. Thus, in far less conspicuous ways, this awesome technological culture is also exploited by dislocated groups to forge new 'imagined' communities, to empower themselves. Kirsten Drotner describes how 'playing' with video can be an empowering experience for young people – a means for girls and boys to explore social and cultural identities through aesthetic production. Finally, Marie Gillespie points to the very important role played by the video recorder in the negotiation of ethnic identities in Britain – a process which can also be found among other ethnic groups (Turks, Moroccans, West Indians) in Europe. In both Drotner's and Gillespie's work we find illuminating examples of the contradictory potentials of the new communication technologies. Drotner implicitly opposes the postmodernist despair over 'the impossibility of politics' by locating the political potential of apparently 'aimless' video production among Danish youth. Similarly, Gillespie shows how, in the community she studied, technology can be seen to play a crucial role in the (re)creation of tradition and in the negotiation of questions of cultural and ethnic identity.

More generally, the issue of ethnicity may prove to be central in the near future of social and cultural life in Europe, when national boundaries may well be more and more dissolved in favour of European integration. As Stuart Hall has noted, 'the question of ethnicity reminds us that everybody comes from some place . . . and needs some sense of identification', whether this be 'in relation to particular communities, localities, territories, languages, religions or cultures' (1988: 29). In the changing economic, political, and cultural landscape of what we are used to call 'Europe', it is the politics of the making (and unmaking) of these identities which the contributors to this issue attempt to address.

University of Amsterdam, the Netherlands,
Brunel University, London, England

Notes

1 This is not to suggest that these tensions are only relevant as between Britain and 'the rest of Europe'. The same championships also produced the sight of jubilant Dutch fans celebrating their team's victory over the Germans as a form of symbolic revenge, not only for their 'undeserved' defeat in the World Cup of 1974, but even more profoundly for the events of World War II.
2 Thus, it is significant that this journal had its origins in Australia. Parallel developments in cultural studies are also taking place in Canada (cf. the magazine *Border/Lines*).
3 Gilroy made his remark during a discussion of postmodernism at the National Film Theatre, London, October 1987.

References

Brunsdon, Charlotte (1989) 'Text and audience'. In Ellen Seiter, Hans Borchers, Gabriele Kreutzner and Eva-Maria Warth (eds), *Remote Control. Television, Audiences and Cultural Power*. London and New York: Routledge.
Centre for Contemporary Cultural Studies (1981) *Unpopular Education*. London: Hutchinson.
Francovits, A. (1987) 'Letters'. *Screen*, 28 (3): 122–4.
Frith, S. (1982) *Sound Effects*: 146, New York: Pantheon.
Gellner, E. (1983) *Nations and Nationalism*. Oxford: Blackwell.

Gilroy, Paul (1986) *There Ain't No Black in the Union Jack*. London: Hutchinson.

Grossberg, Lawrence (1988a) 'Postmodernity and affect: all dressed up with no place to go'. *Communication*, 10 (3/4): 271–93.

Grossberg, Lawrence (1988b) 'Wandering audiences, nomadic critics'. *Cultural Studies*, 2 (3): 377–91.

Hall, Stuart (1986) 'On postmodernism and articulation: an interview with Stuart Hall (edited by Lawrence Grossberg)'. *Journal of Communication Inquiry*, 10 (2): 45–60.

Hall, Stuart (1988) 'Brave new world'. *Marxism Today*, October: 24–9.

Hebdige, Dick (1979) *Subculture: The Meaning of Style*. London: Methuen.

Hebdige, Dick (1988) 'Towards a cartography of taste 1935–1962'. In his *Hiding in the Light*. London and New York: Comedia/Routledge, 45–76.

Luil, James (1988) 'The audience as nuisance'. *Critical Studies in Mass Communication*, 5 (3): 239–43.

Mattelart, Armand, Delcourt, Xavier and Mattelart, Michelle (1984) *International Image Markets*. London: Comedia.

Morris, Meaghan (1987) 'Asleep at the wheel?'. *New Statesman*, 26 June 1987.

Rath, Claus-Dieter (1985) 'The invisible network: television as an institution in everyday life'. In Philip Drummond and Richard Paterson (eds) *Television in Transition*. London: British Film Institute, 199–204.

Schröder, Kim (1988) 'Cultural quality: the search for a phantom?' Paper presented to the International Television Studies Conference, London, July 1988.

Webster, Duncan (1988) *Looka Yonder: the imaginary America of populist culture*. London: Comedia/Routledge.

Willis, Paul (1977) *Learning to Labour*. London: Saxon House.

Willis, Paul (1980) 'Note on method'. In Stuart Hall, Dorothy Hobson, Andrew Lowe and Paul Willis (eds) *Culture, Media, Language*. London: Hutchinson.

KEVIN ROBINS

REIMAGINED COMMUNITIES?
EUROPEAN IMAGE SPACES,
BEYOND FORDISM

> Very much remains to be done by way of detailed dis-
> cussions and proposals, but we cannot in any case live much
> longer under the confusions of the existing 'international'
> economy and the existing 'nation-state'. If we cannot find
> and communicate social forms of more substance than
> these, we shall be condemned to endure the accelerating
> pace of false and frenetic nationalisms and of reckless and
> uncontrollable global transnationalism.
>
> Raymond Williams

> It is invidious to regard places, communities, cities, regions,
> or even nations as 'things in themselves' at a time when the
> global flexibility of capitalism is greater than ever. . . . Yet a
> global strategy of resistance and transformations has to
> begin with the realities of place and community.
>
> David Harvey

A question of geography

In the present period, we are involved with processes of political economic restructuring and transformation, ones that I shall go on to describe in terms of a possible shift beyond that historical system of accumulation and social regulation which has been called Fordism. At the heart of these historical developments – and this is the major concern of the following discussion – is a process of radical spatial restructuring and reconfiguration. It is at once a transformation of the spatial matrix of accumulation and of the subjective experience of, and orientation to, space and spatiality. Its analysis, I want to argue, demands a social theory that is informed by the 'geographical imagination' (Gregory, 1988).

The image industries are implicated in these socio-spatial processes in quite significant and distinctive ways. I want to explore the nature of current transformations, the breaks and continuities, and to assess the implications of the changing configuration of image spaces. Through the prism of geographical analysis it becomes possible to take up some crucial questions concerning the relationship between economic and cultural aspects of these transformations, to explore the articulations of the space of accumulation and cultural spaces. Exploration of these issues must necessarily work through the nature of any relationship between, on the one hand, the transition from Fordism to some (still putative) post-Fordist social system, and, on the other, the trajectory from modernism (and modernity) to postmodernism (and postmodernity). Following this line of enquiry, issues around the politics of communication converge with the politics of space and place: questions of communication are also about the nature and scope of community. In a world of 'false and frenetic nationalisms and of reckless and uncontrollable global transnationalism', the struggle for meaningful communities and 'actual social identities' is more urgent than ever: 'we have to explore new forms of *variable* societies, in which over the whole range of social purposes different sizes of society are defined for different kinds of issue and decision' (Williams, 1983: 198–9).

Beyond Fordism?

What is the broader context within which the transformation of image industries and markets is taking place? One of the most suggestive and productive ways of looking at the present period of upheaval has been that of the Regulation School of political economists (see, *inter alia*, Aglietta, 1979; Billaudot and Gauron, 1985; Boyer, 1986a, 1986b; Lipietz 1987), with their analyses of the decline of the social system of Fordism. Within this perspective, Fordism is understood in terms of the articulation of a particular 'regime of accumulation', centred around mass production and mass consumption, with an appropriate 'mode of regulation'. Social regulation is a matter of both the organizational and institutional structures, particularly the apparatuses of the Keynesian state, but also the norms, habits, and internalized rules governing the lifeworld – the 'architecture of socialisation' (Billaudot and Gauron, 1985: 22) – which ensure social reproduction and the absorption of conflicts and tensions, always provisionally, over a certain period of time. What is being suggested is that Fordism as a mode of capitalist development and, as a historically specific coherence of accumulation and regulation, has now reached its limits. The inherent control problems of Fordism – for example, rising wages and declining productivity, overcapacity and market saturation, competition from low-wage countries, increasing costs for public services (see Roobeek, 1987) – have brought the system into crisis. This crisis, moreover, is structural (rather than simply cyclical), and it is a matter of political, social, and cultural crisis as much as of economic decline and stagnation. Insofar as the resources of Fordism/Keynesianism have become exhausted, the future of capitalist development demands a fundamental and innovative restructuring of accumulation and regulation (Boyer, 1979).

If the historical nature of Fordism and the dynamics of its crisis are becoming clear enough, the question of its successor regime of accumulation is more problematic and contentious. What lies beyond Fordism? There are many accounts of post-Fordism, increasingly congealing into a new orthodoxy of optimism, which identify a new social coherence centred around what is often referred to as an emergent regime of flexible accumulation. So-called flexible specialization is manifest in new forms of decentralized and disseminated production and in design and product mix aimed at niche markets; demassified enterprises abandon economies of scale in favour of economies of scope; and workers supposedly assume new skills and responsibilities and a new sense of autonomy. This perspective finds its apogee in the work of Piore and Sabel (1984) and of other celebrants of the 'Third Italy' and the 'Emilian model' (e.g. Brusco, 1982), who see the transcendence of Fordism in terms of a kind of return to feudalism, with the growth of a new class of artisans and the emergence of localized industrial districts. Whilst there are certain important insights here – and I shall return to them below – there are also strongly ideological elements informing this new myth of flexibility (Gertler, 1988). Post-Fordism is, in effect, imagined as anti-Fordism: it is quite simply the inverse of, and antithesis to, the rigid and massified system of Fordism.

This kind of idealized and teleological account is clearly unsatisfactory. Any real-world transition beyond Fordism will inevitably be a great deal more complex, unruly, and uncertain. As Erica Schoenberger (1988: 260) argues, this is not a matter of some kind of entropic evolutionary movement from one distinct social system to another; it is a process that 'promises to be fraught with turbulence and disruption'. Projected futures cannot simply and effortlessly dissolve away the solidity of inherited social structures, infrastructures and relations. The process of transformation is complex and uneven, and it is genuinely difficult to establish whether the present period marks the emergence of a post-Fordist society, whether it should be characterized as neo-Fordist, or whether, in fact, it remains a period of late Fordism. On what basis is, say, flexible specialization classified as a distinguishing feature of post-Fordism? The basis of definition and periodization is, in fact, not at all self-evident. In a complex process of change, we have to ask by what criteria we might identify the components of a new phase of accumulation, and also how we do so without falling into the trap of teleologism. We must be clear that, in so far as the direction of change will be a matter of struggle and contestation, neither the emergence nor the nature of any society beyond Fordism is predetermined or inevitable.

The present discussion is concerned with one major area of change centring around the nature and meaning of space. What transformations are taking place in the social production of space, place, and spatiality, and what new political logics does this set in motion? My contention is that space is of paramount importance in this period of transition and restructuring: 'the current crisis is *accentuating spatiality* and revealing more clearly than ever before, the spatial and locational strategies of capitalist accumulation and the necessity for labour and all segments of society "peripheralized" by capitalist development and restructuring to create spatially conscious counterstrategies at all geographical scales, in all territorial locales' (Soja, 1985: 188).

Idealizing visions of post-Fordism pick up on this new salience of space, but they do so only very partially. What they perceive is the transmutation of a centralized space economy into new forms of decentralization and dissemination; they emphasize the increasing importance of localized industrial districts and zones like those first described by the economist, Alfred Marshall, early this century (Bellandi, forthcoming). Reality is more complex and contradictory, however. If the growing significance of neo-Marshallian local economic districts is, indeed, an identifiable trend, then there are also apparently countervailing tendencies towards a global network economy. Manuel Castells (1983: 5) has powerfully described how what he calls the informational mode of development, based upon new communications systems and information technologies, is bringing about 'the transformation of spatial *places* into *flows* and *channels* – what amounts to the *delocalization of the processes of production and consumption*'. Castells argues that corporate information networks are underpinning the expansion and integration of the capitalist world system, realizing the possibility of a world assembly line, and opening up truly global markets. 'The new space of a world capitalist system', he argues, 'is a space of variable geometry, formed by locations hierarchically ordered in a continuously changing network of flows' (ibid.: 7). What we are moving towards is a fundamentally delocalized world order articulated around a small number of 'concentrated centres for production of knowledge and storage of information, as well as centres for emission of images and information' (ibid.: 6), nerve centres in the cybernetic grids, command and control headquarters of the world financial and industrial system. The consequence, Castells believes, is 'the formation of a new historical relationship between space and society' (ibid.: 3).

The elaboration of a new spatial order is a consequence, then, of two contrary dynamics. Such complexity has, of course, always characterized the production of space under capitalism. The historical sequence of capitalist spatialities, which has always manifested itself through the geography of uneven territorial development, has been a consequence of the interplay between centripetal and centrifugal forces, between centralization and decentralization, agglomeration and dispersal, homogenization and differentiation. David Harvey (1985) has identified a fundamental developmental logic underpinning this contradictory process. Capital has always sought to overcome spatial barriers and to improve the 'continuity of flow'. It remains the case, however, that spatial constraints always exist and persist in so far as 'capital and labour must be brought together at a particular point in space for production to proceed' (ibid.: 145). Mobility and fixity are integrally and necessarily related: 'The ability of both capital and labour power to move . . . from place to place depends upon the creation of fixed, secure, and largely immobile social and physical infrastructures. The ability to overcome space is predicated on the production of space' (ibid.: 149). There are, then, forces working towards structured coherence and fixity, but also countervailing forces tending towards the simultaneous transcendence and disruption of immobility and coherence; both are moments of the same total process of spatial development.

How, then, is this spatial logic working itself out in the present period of transition? On the basis of new information and communication technologies, capital can now be described as hypermobile and hyperflexible, tending towards deterritorialization and delocalization. But this is not the only characteristic tendency in the present period. Even if capital significantly reduces the friction of geography, it cannot for that escape its dependence on spatial fixity. Space and place cannot be annihilated. As Scott Lash and John Urry (1987: 86) argue, 'the effect of heightened spatial indifference has profound effects upon particular places and upon the forms of life that can be sustained within them – contemporary developments may well be heightening the salience of such localities'. The increasing mobility of corporations is associated with the possibility of fractionalizing and subdividing operations and situating them in different places, and, in the process, taking advantage of small variations in the nature of different localities. The spatial matrix of capitalism in the period beyond Fordism is one that, in fact, combines and articulates tendencies towards both globalization and localization.

These new forms of spatial deployment very much reflect the changing organizational structure of accumulation, and, particularly, new patterns of combined corporate integration and disintegration. One developmental logic of capitalist corporations is towards both horizontal and vertical integration, extending the monopolistic logic of concentration that characterized the Fordist regime of accumulation, and this on an increasingly global scale. This continuing integrative process is complemented however by certain tendencies towards vertical distingration, towards the fragmentation of organizational elements into separate and specialized but functionally interlinked units (see Scott, 1986). This is generally a matter of externalizing non-strategic, specialized, or, perhaps, unpredictable and variable functions and labour processes – and thereby externalizing uncertainty and risk – on the basis of subcontracting or market links.

These emerging organizational transformations take place in and through space and have significant implications for territorial development. As Erik Swyngedouw (1988: 13) emphasizes, vertical disintegration results in the formation of a localized nexus of small units, often centred around one or a few dominant large companies, and involved in 'close contractor/ subcontractor relationships, continuous information exchange and, thus, spatial proximity'. The consequence of this new dynamic of flexible specialization, with its tendencies towards spatial agglomeration, has been to give a new centrality to local economies (Courlet and Judet, 1986). It is at the level of locality that important new economic and social dynamics are being worked out. It is precisely this aspect of organizational–territorial transformation that the idealizing champions of post-Fordist industrial districts have identified as decisive. They do so in a rather one-sided way, however, disarticulating the local from its global framework. Territorial complexes of quasi-integrated organizations are extremely vulnerable to external disruptions inflicted by globally mobile and footloose corporations: 'The evolution of flexibility within corporations . . . means that places are created and used up more quickly for the purposes of production or consumption' (Thrift, 1987: 211).

In a context in which 'regions "implode" into localities and nations "explode" into a complex global space' (Albertsen, 1986: 4–5), we have, then, an increasingly direct relationship between the local and the global. And as part of this process, it should be emphasized, the role and significance of the nation-state has become ever more problematical and questionable (though no less ambitious). As Raymond Williams (1983: 197) argues, 'it is now very apparent, in the development of modern industrial societies, that the nation-state, in its classical European forms, is at once too large and too small for the range of real social purposes'. The politics of space and place is now a fundamental issue. The question, in the present period, is whether national and nationalist identities can be transcended in favour of more meaningful identities, or whether they will simply transform in regressive and alienating ways. For Manuel Castells (1983: 4), the prospects are bleak: 'On the one hand, the space of power is being transformed into flows. On the other hand, the space of meaning is being reduced to microterritories of new tribal communities'. He envisages a new 'space of collective alienation', one in which there is a 'deconnection between people and spatial form', 'the outer experience is cut off from the inner experience' (ibid.: 7). Castells' prognosis should not be taken lightly. But does the present situation contain other, progressive and hopeful possibilities?

Image spaces, beyond Fordism?

These processes of socio-spatial transformation are the essential context for understanding the nature and significance of developments in the audiovisual industries. In this section and the next I want to look at the developing relationship between globalization and localization specifically in terms of the logics at work in the audiovisual industries. I want to reorientate the politics of communication towards a politics of space and place. What is the nature of emerging new image markets and image spaces, and what significance do these have for 'imaginary space' (Garnier, 1987), the sense of space and the sense of place? The context for the restructuring of image spaces is the very clear crisis of public service regulation, the broadcasting system elaborated under European Fordism/Keynesianism, with its focus on the national arena and nationalist identities. The crisis is likely to be protracted. Thus, whilst it is increasingly clear that technological and economic transformations are surpassing the regulatory capacities of the nation-state, there is, at the ideological level, still an obsessive and regressive 'desire to reproduce the nation that has died and the moral and social certainties which have vanished with it . . . to fudge and forge a false unity based on faded images of the nation' (MacCabe, 1988: 29). National ambitions and endeavours will not simply disappear. In this context, none the less, what scope is there for intervention between the global and the local? If there is to be a post-Fordist media system, in what image will it be created? Castells (1983: 16) fears the worst: 'the coexistence both of the monopoly of messages by the big networks and of the increasingly narrow codes of local microcultures around their parochial cable TVs'. Is the prospect necessarily and inevitably one of increasing privatism, localism, and 'cultural tribalism' within an electronic global village?

To begin to answer this question, we must look at the new media industries in terms of the complex dynamics of restructuring that we have already discussed in more general terms, particularly the interplay between globalization and localization. What is most apparent and remarkable is the accelerating formation of global communications empires, such as those of Murdoch, Maxwell, Berlusconi, or Bertelsmann. Internationalization is not, of course, a new phenomenon; it was very much a constitutive aspect of Fordist development. But it is now entering a new stage, and the 'maintenance of national sovereignty and identity are becoming increasingly difficult as the unities of economic and cultural production and consumption become increasingly transnational' (Collins, Garnham and Locksley, 1988: 55). We are seeing the emergence of truly global, decentred, corporations in which diverse media products (film and television, press and publishing, music and video) are being combined into overarching communications empires. Co-financed and co-produced products are made on a global assembly line and are aimed at world markets. Out of a context of collapsing public service traditions, and the consequent deregulation of national broadcasting systems, these mega-corporations are shaping a global space of image flows.

This process of globalization is very much a function of increasing corporate integration. Various forms of horizontal alignment are apparent, at both national and international levels, with new alliances between broadcasters, film and television producers, publishers, record producers, and so on. But as a recent Logica report (1987: 131) makes very clear, it is 'the emergence of new media groups on a vertically integrated scale [that] is the single most important factor in the nature and spread of commercial TV development in Europe'. The progression of Rupert Murdoch, through Fox Broadcasting, 20th Century Fox, and Sky Channel, towards the achievement of integrated control over production, distribution, and broadcasting is simply the most obvious example. Logica (ibid.: 268–70) identifies the main functions in the chain of television production as those of originator, programmer, broadcaster, carrier, and network operator, and it argues that new media groups 'are aiming to achieve vertical integration over some or all of the above roles'. Total integration is, in fact, likely to be less significant, and less attainable, than the strategic integration of particular functions, and Logica identifies those of carrier/broadcaster, broadcaster/programmer, and programmer/originator as critical to the consolidation of power blocs in the communications industries.

The tendency towards vertical integration is not, then, absolute and encompassing. Indeed, as with the transformation of accumulation beyond

Fordism more generally, it is also, in fact, combined with processes of vertical disintegration. Thus, in the case of the American motion picture industry, Michael Storper and Susan Christopherson (1987) suggest that whilst the major studios control and dominate finance, product definition, distribution, and marketing, there has been a clear move towards the externalization of production and the use of small independent producers. This process of deverticalization is associated with both the externalization of risk and the attempt to exploit maximum variety of creative resources. One significant consequence has been a distinctive new pattern of location: independent producers have become spatially concentrated 'because the specialised nature of their services and the constant change in product requires non-routine, frequent market transactions with other firms, such as production companies and major studios' (Christopherson and Storper, 1986: 316). The instability of casualized employment relations and the importance of contact networks generate significant agglomeration tendencies at a local level.

There are many who see this trend towards vertical disintegration and territorial localization as heralding a benign post-Fordist era of flexible specialization and cultural industrial districts. It is important, however, to emphasize that vertical disintegration applies primarily to the production sector. As Nicholas Garnham (1986: 31–2) argues: '*It is cultural distribution, not cultural production, that is the key locus of power and profit. It is access to distributions which is the key to cultural plurality.*' Given its strategic importance, the function of distribution is not likely to be externalized. It is also important to emphasize that the logics of integration and disintegration are not contradictory, but, rather, quite complementary. Whilst disintegration and localization are important however, as I shall go on to argue, integration and globalization remain the dominant and embracing forces.

The evolution of localized media production has become a significant issue in Europe, too (Rabaté, 1987), assuming distinct and particular forms in specific national and regional contexts. The case of Britain offers a good example of partial vertical disintegration and, particularly, of its ambiguous and contradictory political implications. Whereas previously the functions of production, editorial and repertoire, and distribution, had been integrated in British broadcasting, with the opening of Channel 4 in 1982 there was a move towards their disaggregation. As with the American film industry, the key innovation was the externalization of programme-making, which had as its consequence the growth and consolidation of a small-business sector of independent producers. Many of these companies, often involved in politically radical projects, located their activities away from the metropolitan centre, forming into small and localized agglomerations in regional cities (such as Cardiff, Newcastle, Bristol, Leeds, Manchester, Birmingham). These developments succoured real hopes and anticipations for the deconcentration, decentralization and democratization of the audiovisual industries. Over the past months, a second wave of deverticalization has begun to emerge, in the context of the government's decision, following the recommendations of the Peacock Report, that both the BBC and the ITV companies should subcontract 25 per cent of their programmes to independent producers. This new wave of transformation, however, severely undercuts idealizing expectations and projections. It is increasingly clear that externalization and subcontracting of production is creating, not 'independent' and autonomous programme-makers, but a casualized, segmented, and precarious workforce. This creation of an external workforce is, above all, part of a strategy to break the 'restrictive practices' of the broadcasting unions. 'Flexible working deals', such as those being imposed by Tyne Tees, London Weekend Television, TV-AM and Thames Television, are aimed at asserting discipline and control over employees and thereby, of course, strengthening profitability and comparative advantage. Flexibility translates into power: through new contractual relations with internal employees and through the power of market relations with external subcontractors. So-called flexible specialization combines organizational and functional disintegration or disaggregation with the continued integration of control and co-ordination.

What, we must now ask, are the political implications of these combined processes of integration and disintegration, globalization and localization? What is, in fact, emerging is a certain displacement of national frameworks in ‑favour of perspectives and agendas appropriate to both supra-national and sub-national dynamics. In this process, new questions are being thrown up about the interrelation of spaces of accumulation, on the one hand, and arenas of cultural consumption and cultural identity, on the other.

The global politics of communication centres around the international 'war of images', the struggle between 'image superpowers' (Frèches, 1986). This war of position between transnational corporations is reflected very strongly in the concerns of the Commission of the European Communities. In a world swamped by television images, the key questions are 'Where will these pictures come from? Who will capture the market – and the employment – for producing and transmitting them?' (Commission of the European Communities, 1986: 3). If American dominance is to be challenged, it is argued, then a pan-European industry and market is imperative: the common market in electronics and aerospace products 'must create conditions for economies of scale to allow European industries to produce in greater quantities, at the lowest possible price, and to recoup their investment costs' (Commission of the European Communities, 1988: 3). Technical progress is now 'making a mockery of frontiers', and 'the day of purely national audiences, markets and channels is gone': the logic of development must be towards a 'European audio-visual area' (Commission of the European Communities, 1986: 3). In default of this, it is feared that European audiovisual markets are likely to be dominated by the output of American, Japanese, or Brazilian corporations.

This strategy is very much aimed at supporting, and integrating, large European corporations. Open skies and network flows are seen as fundamental to the creation of a single large market that will underpin a European industrial and economic renaissance. In this context, 'television without frontiers' (Commission of the European Communities, 1984) is also very much implicated in opening up global advertising markets and spaces. As yet, 'the restrictions and constraints on television advertising across Europe mean that the television set is still relatively unexploited as an advertising medium' (Tydeman and Kelm, 1986: 63). The future of the image industries is very much imbricated in that of global advertising: a European audiovisual area is intended to support and facilitate 'freedom of commercial speech in Europe' (Hondius, 1985).

This pan European space of accumulation is also projected as a space of culture and identity: 'the creation of a large market establishes a European area based on common cultural roots as well as social and economic realities' (Commission of the European Communities, 1987: 3). It is a matter of 'maintaining and promoting the cultural identity of Europe', of 'improving mutual knowledge among our peoples and increasing their consciousness of the life and destiny they have in common' (Commission of the European Communities, 1988: 3, 11). A transnational politics of culture is worked out in terms of the articulation of European affiliations and allegiances as against, particularly, an Atlanticist cultural identity. But there are problems about what such a 'people's Europe' might be. What is the meaning of this 'sense of belonging to a community composed of countries which are different yet partake of a deep solidarity' (ibid.: 4)? Is it possible to translate a multinational administrative unity into any meaningful identity and solidarity? Perhaps it is the differences, what the Commission (1986: 8) recognizes as 'richness' and 'cultural diversity', which are more significant in the creation of positive attachments and identities? What must be recognized is that there are forces also working against cultural homogenization and transnationalism. In the context of centripetal tendencies brought about by the globalization of communications, there are also centrifugal tendencies 'to protect and preserve native languages and cultures' (Gifreu, 1986: 465). The 'globalisation of social transactions', experienced as an 'internationalisation process, which is gradually robbing Europe of its originality and demobilising its citizens, so that European cultural differences are disintegrating' (Bassand, 1988: 2–3), also produces localized and particularized communities and identities.

Working both against and within a supra-national politics of communication and culture, there is a growing sub-national agenda focused around local and urban cultural identities. Local media are now increasingly being seen as 'regional-building tools not only in traditional cultural terms (regional awareness, cultural identity, linguistic crystallisation), but also in terms of economy (provision of jobs, sensitisation of the public to communication technologies, dynamisation of local markets, etc.)' (Crookes and Vittet-Philippe, 1986: 4). As Torsten Hägerstrand (1986: 10, 16, 18) argues, in the context of a system society, in which many activities have 'released themselves from the bonds and fetters of place, and in which the media 'have contributed very little to the local and regional content of world-pictures', there arise countervailing tendencies to explore the 'possibility space' of local media, to establish localized arenas for public debate and cultural expression, to elaborate, in fact, meaningful local public spheres.

The case of Britain is again instructive. Tendencies in the organization of the audiovisual industries towards partial disintegration and the externalization of production, have, in a society historically characterized by a 'national' framework of centralized and metropolitan cultural influence (Robson, 1986), become associated with the elaboration of significant local cultural initiatives. In a number of urban and local contexts, the image industries have been at the forefront of local economic and cultural restructuring. Glasgow ('European City of Culture'), Sheffield, Birmingham, Liverpool, Newcastle, Bradford, Cardiff ('Media City') have been prominent in launching important initiatives. Important policy statements have put forward strategies for a cultural industries quarter (Centre for Popular Culture, 1988), for a media development agency, a media centre, and a media zone (Comedia, 1987; Birmingham City Council, 1988), and, in the case of Nottingham, an Audiovisual-Fashion-Information Technology triangle (Nottingham Media Consortium, 1987). Following the model of the Greater London Council in the early 1980s, these strategies move towards the elaboration of localized cultural industrial districts, along neo-Marshallian lines. In many cases, this question of local industrial and cultural public spheres raises questions about public space, and issues of the quality of working and leisure time become translated into policies for the urban fabric and the design of the built environment (see Worpole, Morley, and Southwood, 1987).

It is not simply a story of economic and cultural radicalization, however: the local sphere is a contested terrain. The culture of locality is not only a concern of progressive authorities; it is also high on the agenda of communications conglomerates seeking to combine global marketing with the targeting of local and regional consumers. The cultural industries are not just about programme-making, but also and crucially about distribution, and so long as the new conduits of distribution, such as cable and microwave systems, are closed to democratic access, then aspirations for cultural radicalism will remain an empty ideal.

Local initiatives have also been shaped by external political intervention; local autonomy and accountability have been undermined by centrally-imposed development strategies. Whilst 'the official story from the centre has been one of rolling back the state and freedom from bureaucratic control', it is in fact the case that 'the "market freedom" supposedly represented by Free Enterprise Zones and Urban Development Corporations is supported by an almost unprecedented level of state subsidy and support' (Duncan and Goodwin, 1988: 272). We have apparently moved a long way from the local socialism of the Greater London Council to the present government's 'enterprise strategy' for cities with its 'philosophy of open markets and individuals' (Department of Trade and Industry, 1988). But what we have in the development corporations' combined strategies for industry, leisure, and the urban fabric, is an opportunist inflection and incorporation of that earlier localist politics. And the arts and cultural industries are being drawn into the heart of this entrepreneurial initiative. Cable is envisaged as a means 'to tackle multifarious difficulties being faced in inner city areas and to achieve successful regeneration' (Cable Authority, 1987). And, according to the Arts Council (1988: 2), the arts 'are essential ingredients in the mix of cultural, environmental and recreational amenities which reinforce economic growth and development. They attract tourism and the jobs it brings. More importantly, they can serve as the main catalyst for the wholesale regeneration of an area. They provide focal points for community pride and identity'.

The new culture of enterprise enlists the enterprise of culture to manufacture differentiated urban or local identities. These are centred around the creation of an image, a fabricated and inauthentic identity, a false aura, usually achieved through 'the recuperation of "history" (real, imagined, or simply re-created as pastiche) and of "community" (again, real, imagined, or simply packaged for sale by producers)' (Harvey, 1987: 274). The context for this is the increased pressure on cities and localities, in the conditions of accumulation emerging beyond Fordism, to adopt an entrepreneurial stance in order to attract mobile global capital. The marketing of local identities and images as a function of intensified inter-urban competition, and success, as David Harvey (1987: 278) argues, 'is often short-lived or rendered moot by competing or alternative innovations arising elsewhere'. Under such conditions, local economies are precarious and local identities and cultures may be false and fragile.

Postmodern spaces, reimagined communities?

> We must therefore begin to think of cultural politics in terms of space and the struggle for space.
>
> Fredric Jameson

So far, I have approached recent developments in the audiovisual industries in terms of broader transformations of the dominant regime of accumulation, beyond Fordism. In this context, I have emphasized particularly the new geographical logics shaping and informing audiovisual cultures. What is most apparent here is the dual tendency towards both globalization and localization of image spaces. Clearly, the global forces overshadow and overawe the local, though, as David Gordon (1988) emphasizes, transnational corporations are not all-powerful and they have yet to achieve global co-ordination and control. The outcome of current upheavals is not determinate. Post-Fordist cultural industries could assume a number of quite different forms, and the interrelation between global and local processes could vary considerably. The point here is to identify the logics shaping emergent image spaces, and thereby the parameters within which political and policy initiatives make sense.

I want now to approach these same processes from a different perspective, to look at the audiovisual sector in the context of broader *cultural* transformations, beyond modernism. What does it mean to talk of the postmodernization of European cultures and identities? Many commentators have assumed a symmetrical, and often causal, relationship between a projected transition to post-Fordism and a transition to postmodernism. And they have done so in terms of a periodizing hypothesis, a stage theory of social development, in which one historical phase is abruptly succeeded by another. The reality is more complex, however. The logics of post-Fordism and postmodernism are clearly articulated, but the postmodernization process, working through a longer historical temporality, is also about a more fundamental transformation associated with the crisis of the Enlightenment project. And it is very much a transformation *in process*: the nature of postmodern culture and society is still a matter of speculation and contestation. As Blaise McBurney (1985: 96) writes, 'postmodernism is something to be struggled for'; the operative question is not 'What is postmodernism?', but rather 'What should postmodernism be?'. The apocalyptic tone of most postmodern culture in the present period reflects a sense of crisis and ending: as a more active and anticipatory force, the postmodern remains to be imagined.

As with post-Fordism, I want to focus my discussion by looking at postmodernism as a question of geography. Where the modernist imagination was centred around questions of time and duration, postmodernism is preoccupied with space and spatiality. As Fredric Jameson argues, 'the locus of our new reality and the cultural politics by which it must be confronted is that of space' (Stephanson, 1987: 40). This concerns spatial processes and structures, but also the subjective side of space, orientation within space, and experience of space. And it is also a matter of both global space and local space: 'what is wanted is . . . a new relationship between a global cultural style and the specificity and demands of a concrete local or national situation' (ibid.). How do we position ourselves within the new global cultural space? How do we reconcile our cognitive existence in hyperspace, in the virtual space of electronic networks, with our bodily existence in localized space? Can we reposition ourself in local space without falling into nostalgic sentiments of community and *Gemeinschaft*? In Raymond Williams' (1983) terms, what new forms of bonding are possible and appropriate? What can community be made to mean in a postmodern society?

Most contemporary discussions of postmodernism are concerned with the disorientating experience of global space, and fundamental to this concern is the impact of global image space. Richard Kearney (1988: 1–2) describes a world in which the image reigns supreme, a 'Civilization of the Image' in which 'reality has become a pale reflection of the image. . . . The real and the imaginary have become almost impossible to distinguish'. With 'the omnipresence of self destructing images which simulate each other in a limitless interplay of mirrors', argues Kearney, 'the psychic world is as colonised as the physical world by the whole image industry' (ibid.: 5, 1). If this globalization of image flows and spaces is fundamentally transforming spatiality and sense of space, it is also, through its impact on architecture and the built environment, transforming the nature and sense of place. Thus, postmodern Los Angeles is, according to Mike Davis (1987: 67), 'a city where architecture and electronic image have fused into a single hyperspace'. John Portman's Bonaventure hotel has been taken as a symbol of this postmodernization of urban form. Its 'great reflective glass skin achieves a peculiar and placeless dissociation of the Bonaventure from its neighbour-hood': 'the distorting and fragmentary reflection of one enormous glass surface to the other can be taken as paradigmatic of the central role of process and reproduction in postmodern culture'. This new decentred and global world of images, surfaces, simulacra, creates new experiences of space. Jameson (see Stephanson, 1987: 33) refers to the 'existential be-wilderment in this new postmodern space', a 'culture in which one cannot position oneself'.

This aspect of postmodernization is most apparent, perhaps, in the writings of Jean Baudrillard. In the society of the image, he argues, the individual is 'now only a pure screen, a switching centre for all the networks of influence' (Baudrillard, 1985: 133). With the television image, 'our own body and the whole surrounding universe become a control screen': 'the simple presence of the television changes the rest of the habitat into a kind of archaic envelope, a vestige of human relations whose very survival remains perplexing . . . as soon as behaviour is crystallised on certain screens and operational terminals, what's left appears only as a large useless body, deserted and condemned' (ibid.: 129). This is the world of screen and network, the 'smooth operational surface of communication': a world of 'absolute proximity, the total instantaneity of things, the feeling of no defence, no retreat' (ibid.: 133).

This postmodern hyperspace is very much the cultural echo of that logic of transnational networks and communication flows which Manuel Castells sees as characterizing the globalization and cybernation of accumulation. However, whilst Castells (1983: 4) sees the consequence of this as 'the destruction of human experience, therefore of communication, and there-fore of society', Baudrillard (1985: 132) comes to celebrate 'a state of fascination and vertigo linked to this obscene delirium of communication'. He is seduced by the new communications networks, by the information and image flows, and by the decentred and disorientated identities associated with them. This new space of flows is shaped and controlled by transnatio-nal capital: it is the space of IBM and AT&T, of Murdoch and Berlusconi. It is their evolving network marketplace of commodity flows and advertising spectacle that generates Baudrillard's 'ecstasy of communication'. It is their screens and networks and simulations and cybernetic systems that produce his cybernetic awe and sense of the technological sublime.

Postmodern culture in Baudrillard's sense does, of course, engage with important developments in the late twentieth century: 'It is articulating something that is going on. If the subject is lost in it, and if in social life the psychic subject has been decentred by late capitalism, then this art faithfully and authentically registers it. That's its moment of truth' (Stephanson, 1987: 39). We should not devalue this moment of truth. It may even be exhilarating to know it. But, the point must be to push it further. As Richard

Kearney (1988: 380) argues, 'it is not sufficient to merely *know* that the technological colonisation of images is a symptom of a globally computered network of "third stage" multinational capital'. Knowing this, we must ask a more difficult question: 'Where are we to find a place of critical distance where we may begin to imagine alternative projects of social existence capable of counteracting the paralysis which the "technological sublime" induces in us?'

What is significant about this kind of postmodernist culture and theory is its preoccupation with mediation: image, simulation, network, screen, simulation, spectacle. Marike Finlay (quoted in Young, 1988: 9), suggests that postmodernism is 'a psychotic defence against the loss of referential identity'. Technological mediation is associated with estrangement from the real. In philosophical terms, this psychotic derealization is an ultimate consequence of the logic of scientific and administrative rationality, the totalizing ambitions of abstract and formal reason. In more social terms, it is a 'culturally generalized psychosis' appropriate to a rationalized, bureau-cratic, and technocratic society of indirect relationships and large-scale system integration, now on a global scale; a society in which space-transcending information and communication technologies allow 'the creation of organisations sufficiently complex and "impersonal" that they are readily reified', and conceived 'not as products of human action but as autonomous systems' (Calhoun, 1988: 5).

Rationalization in both its bureaucratic and psychotic forms is char-acterized by what Michael Rustin (1987: 31) calls abstract universalism, with its 'denial of the particular location of human lives in place and time', its placeless and non-referential sense of identity. Rustin argues that cultural and political intervention beyond modernism needs, rather, to take account of social texture, density, difference. In this sense, a postmodern theory would counter, against the abstract universalism of modernity, 'a new particularism', a 'recognition that collective identities are formed through the common occupancy of space, and are constituted in relations of particularist kinds' (ibid.: 34). In this sense, postmodernism is about the (post-Enlightenment) reclamation, or reimagination, of a sense of referential identity, the revaluation of concrete and particular experience. And it is about the elaboration of a new form of collective subjectivity, 'decentred but not schizophrenic' (Stephanson, 1987: 45). In Richard Rorty's (1985: 3) terms, it is about solidarity, as opposed to objectivity, as a way of placing one's life in a larger context. According to the Enlightenment ideal of objectivity, the individual 'distances himself [*sic*] from the actual persons around him . . . by attaching himself to something which can be described without reference to any particular human beings'. The desire for solidarity, on the other hand, is referential and contextualized: the individual tells the story of his or her contribution to a community, be it 'the actual historical one in which they live, or another actual one, distant in time or place, or a quite imaginary one'. This process of bonding can occur in the context of attachment to bounded territorial locations, though it should not be thought that this is about an ambition to return to the parochial world of

Gemeinschaft. Under the conditions of postmodernity, the local cannot be severed from the global; simply to 'identify the local with the politically reactionary is to miss the essential revolution in the relationship of the local and the global in this *fin de siècle*' (Storper, 1987: 425). But solidarity and collectivity must also have aspirations directed beyond the locality. In terms of the global image space, Richard Kearney (1988: 387–8) calls for 'a practice of imagination capable of responding to the postmodern call of the other reaching towards us from the mediatised gaze':

> On the far side of the self-reflecting looking glass, beyond the play of masks and mirrors, there are human beings who suffer and struggle, live and die, hope and despair. Even in those televisual images which transmit events from the furthest corners of our globe, we are being addressed, potentially at least, by living others. . . . Are not those of us who witness such images . . . obliged to respond not just to surface reflections on a screen but to the call of human beings they communicate?

What does this mean for European identities? Refuge in some simple and coherent national, and nationalist, identity cannot be easily sustained. In a European context, at least, what Benedict Anderson (1983) calls the 'imagined communities' of nationalism are increasingly problematical. Whilst a protracted and fierce rearguard action will, no doubt, be waged in the embittered defence of nations and nationhood, it is clear that socio-spatial transformations in the late twentieth century call for new orientations and new forms of bonding. The most obvious response to these new conditions has, of course, been the attempt to build a European Community: a 'common market', a 'citizens' Europe', a 'Europe of culture'. The attempt to cope with simultaneous fragmentation and globalization here produces a political compromise whereby national cultures are subsumed and preserved in a spurious, administrative–bureaucratic inter-nationalism. Defined as it is against the American and Japanese threats, this really amounts to a kind of supra-nationalism (and perhaps super-nationalism?).

But what, then, are the conditions and requirements for genuinely reimagined communities? As Raymond Williams argues in *Towards 2000*, we must explore new forms of variable societies and variable identities. Postmodern culture must be elaborated out of differential and plural identities, rather than collapsing into some false cohesion and unity. It must be about positions and positioning in local *and* global space: about contexts of bodily existence and about existence in mediated space. At one level, it is about bounded and localized spatial arenas which bring individuals into direct social contact, about revaluing public places and recreating a civic culture. But is must also be recognized, as Craig Calhoun (1988: 27–8) argues, that 'however desirable decentralised communities might be, they are at most complements to system integration and not alternatives to it'. It is necessary to improve the way large-scale systems work, and this means learning how to use the mass media and the new information technologies to create 'a new forum for public discourse'.

Much of this discussion has emphasized the stifling power of global image corporations. However, emergent transformations in the space of accumulation and in the spatial disposition of cultural forms, do open up some important new possibilities for reimagined solidarities. The recent growth in decentralized programme-making opens up the possibility of local media spaces. It is possible to envisage 'an amplification of the internal flows of communication in regions and localities' that might 'establish platforms for public debate and distinctive cultural expression' (Hägerstrand, 1986: 18). Public discourse, grounded in a spatial framework, could be elaborated in a local public sphere. In this context, audiovisual culture must be seen as part of a much broader strategy for local development through the stimulation of cultural innovation, identity, and difference (Bassand *et al.*, 1986). Whilst such localism could, of course, degenerate into the introverted and nostalgic historicism and heritage fixation that characterizes a certain kind of conservative postmodernism, local attachment can be seen in more radical and innovative terms. New conditions of mobility make local attachment, not a matter of ascribed and determined identity, but increasingly a question of choice, decision and variability. Local cultures are, moreover, permeated and suffused by external influences. As Kenneth Frampton argues, local cultures can only be constituted now as locally inflected manifestations of global culture. What is called for, in his view, is a strategy of Critical Regionalism 'to mediate the impact of universal civilisation with elements derived indirectly from the peculiarities of a particular place' (Frampton, 1985: 21). A critical regional or local culture must necessarily be in dialogue with global culture.

But postmodern identities must also be about internationalism in a direct sense, about our positions in transnational and transcultural spaces. At one level, this can be a matter of supra-national language and cultural communities: of, for example, 'francophone identities' (Jouanny, 1988) or, more radically, a 'latin audiovisual space' (Mattelart, Delcourt, and Mattelart, 1984). But it must also transcend a Eurocentric perspective to other forms of dialogue and collectivity. Fundamental here are solidarities with Third World cultures: those outside Europe, but also the Third World communities, in all their diversity, now installed within European territories. European identity can no longer be, simply and unproblematically, a matter of western intellectual and cultural traditions. As a consequence of its belligerent, imperialistic, and colonialist history, Europe now contains a rich diversity of cultures and identities. The question is whether ethnic (and also gendered) differences are disavowed and repressed, or whether they can be accepted – and accepted, moreover, in their difference. As Derek Gregory (1988: 4) argues, acceptance must be in the spirit of 'comprehending the "otherness" of other cultures' and of revaluing the specificities of places and of people. 'There are', he emphasizes, 'few tasks more urgent in a multi-cultural society and an interdependent world'.

University of Newcastle Upon Tyne, England

References

Aglietta, Michel (1979) *A Theory of Capitalist Regulation: The US Experience.* London: New Left Books.

Albertsen, Niels (1986) 'Towards post-Fordist localities? An essay on the socio-spatial restructuring process in Denmark'. Paper presented to the XIth World Congress of Sociology, New Delhi, August.

Andserson, Benedict (1983) *Imagined Communities: Reflections on the Origins and Spread of Nationalism.* London. Verso.

Arts Council (1988) *An Urban Renaissance.* London: Arts Council of Great Britain.

Bassand, Michel (1988) 'Communication in cultural and regional development'. Paper presented to the Conference on Society, Information and Space, Department of Geography, Swiss Federal Institute of Technology, Zürich, 21–2 January.

Bassand, Michel, Hainard, François, Pedrazzini, Yves, Perrinjaquet, Roger (1986) *Innovation et Changement Social: Actions Culturelles pour un Développement Local.* Lausanne: Presses Polytechniques Romandes.

Baudrillard, Jean (1985) 'The ecstasy of communication'. In Hal Foster (ed.) *Postmodern Culture.* London: Pluto, 126–36.

Bellandi, Marco (1989) 'The Marshallian industrial district'. In Edward Goodman (ed.) *Small Firms and Industrial Districts in Italy.* London: Routledge.

Billaudot, Bernard and Gauron, André (1985) *Croissance et Crise: Vers une Nouvelle Croissance.* 2nd edn. Paris: La Découverte.

Birmingham City Council (1988) *Media Development Agency Prospectus.* Birmingham: Birmingham City Council.

Boyer, Robert (1979) 'La crise actuelle: une mise en perspective historique'. *Critiques de L'Economie Politique*, 7/8: 5–113.

Boyer, Robert (1986a) *La Théorie de la Regulation: Une Analyse Critique.* Paris: La Découverte.

Boyer, Robert (1986b) *Capitalismes Fin de Siècle.* Paris: Presses Universitaires de France.

Brusco, Sebastiano (1982) 'The Emilian model: productive decentralisation and social integration'. *Cambridge Journal of Economics*, 6: 167–84.

Cable Authority (1987) *Cable and the Inner Cities.* London: Cable Authority.

Calhoun, Craig (1988) 'Communications technology and the transformation of the urban public sphere'. Paper presented to the International Conference on Information, Technology and the New Meaning of Space, International Sociological Association, Research Committee 24, Frankfurt, 15–19 May.

Castells, Manuel (1983) 'Crisis, planning, and the quality of life: managing the new historical relationships between space and society'. *Society and Space*, 1 (1): 3–21.

Centre for Popular Culture, Sheffield City Polytechnic (1988) *Cultural Industries: Interim Report No. 1.* Sheffield: Sheffield City Council.

Christopherson, Susan, and Storper, Michael (1986) 'The city as studio; the world as back lot: The impact of vertical disintegration on the location of the motion picture industry'. *Society and Space*, 4 (3): 305–20.

Collins, Richard, Garnham, Nicholas, and Locksley, Gareth (1988) *The Economics of Television: UK Case.* London: Sage.

Comedia (1987) *Birmingham Audio-Visual Industry: Feasibility Study.* Birmingham: Birmingham City Council.

Commission of the European Communities (1984) *Television Without Frontiers.* Brussels: Commission of the European Communities.

Commission of the European Communities (1986) 'Television and the audio-visual sector: towards a European policy'. *European File,* 14/86 (August–September).

Commission of the European Communities (1987) *A Fresh Boost for Culture in the European Community.* Brussels: Commission of the European Communities.

Commission of the European Communities (1988) 'Towards a large European audio-visual market'. *European File,* 4/88 (February).

Courlet, Claude and Judet, Pierre (1986) 'Nouveaux espaces de production en France et en Italie'. *Annales de la Recherche Urbaine,* 29: 95–103.

Crookes, Philip and Vittet-Philippe, Patrick (1986) *Local Radio and Regional Development in Europe.* Manchester: European Institute for the Media.

Davis, Mike (1985) '*Chinatown,* part two? The "internationalisation" of downtown Los Angeles'. *New Left Review,* 164: 65–86.

Department of Trade and Industry (1988) *DTI – The Department for Enterprise.* Cm 278. London: HMSO.

Duncan, Simon and Goodwin, Mark (1988) *The Local State and Uneven Development: Behind the Local Government Crisis.* Cambridge: Polity Press.

Frampton, Kenneth (1985) 'Towards a critical regionalism: six points for an architecture of resistance'. In Hal Foster (ed.) *Postmodern Culture.* London: Pluto, 16–30.

Frèches, José (1986) *La Guerre des Images.* Paris: Denoël.

Garnham, Nicholas (1986) 'Concepts of culture: public policy and the cultural industries'. *Cultural Studies,* 1 (1): 23–37.

Garnier, Jean-Pierre (1987) 'L'espace médiatique ou l'utopie localisée'. *Espaces et Sociétés,* 50: 7–21.

Gertler, Meric S. (1988) 'The limits to flexibility: Comments on the post-Fordist vision of production and its geography'. Paper presented to the Annual Meeting of the Association of American Geographers, Phoenix, Arizona, 8 April.

Gifreu, Josep (1986) 'From communication policy to reconstruction of cultural identity'. *European Journal of Communication,* 1 (4): 463–76.

Gordon, David M. (1988) 'The global economy: new edifice or crumbling foundations?' *New Left Review,* 168: 24–64.

Gregory, Derek (1988) 'Difference, distance and post-modern human geography'. Unpublished manuscript, Department of Geography, University of Cambridge.

Hägerstrand, Torsten (1986) 'Decentralization and radio broadcasting: on the "possibility space" of a communication technology'. *European Journal of Communication,* 1 (1): 7–26.

Harvey, David (1985) 'The geopolitics of capitalism'. In Derek Gregory and John Urry (eds) *Social Relations and Social Structures.* London: Macmillan, 128–63.

Harvey, David (1987) 'Flexible accumulation through urbanization: reflections on "post-modernism" in the American city'. *Antipode,* 19 (3): 260–86.

Hondius, Frits W. (1985) 'Freedom of commercial speech in Europe'. *Transnational Data Report,* 8 (6): 321–7.

Jameson, Fredric (1984) 'Postmodernism, or the cultural logic of late capitalism'. *New Left Review,* 146: 53–92.

Jouanny, Robert (1988) 'Espaces et identités francophones'. *Acta Geographica,* 73: 13–23.

Kearney, Richard (1988) *The Wake of Imagination: Ideas of Creativity in Western Culture.* London: Hutchinson.

Lash, Scott and Urry, John (1987) *The End of Organized Capitalism*. Cambridge: Polity Press.

Lipietz, Alain (1987) *Mirages and Miracles: The Crises of Global Fordism*. London: Verso.

Logica (1987) *Television Broadcasting in Europe: Towards the 1990s*. London: Logica Consultancy Ltd.

McBurney, Blaise (1985) 'The post-modern transvaluation of modernist values'. *Thesis Eleven*, 12: 94–109.

MacCabe, Colin (1988) 'Those golden years'. *Marxism Today*, 32 (4).

Mattelart, Armand, Delcourt, Xavier and Mattelart, Michele (1984) *International Image Markets*. London: Comedia.

Nottingham Media Consortium (1987) *Audiovisual Information Industries and the Local Economy*. Nottingham: Nottingham Media Consortium.

Piore, Michael J. and Sabel, Charles F. (1984) *The Second Industrial Divide: Possibilities for Prosperity*. New York: Basic.

Rabaté, François (1987) 'La production "locale" de l'audiovisuel'. *Espaces et Sociétés*, 50: 23–68.

Robson, Brian (1986) 'Coming full circle: London versus the rest 1890–1980'. In George Gordon (ed.) *Regional Cities in the U.K., 1890–1980*. London: Harper & Row.

Rorty, Richard (1985) 'Solidarity or objectivity?' In John Rajchman and Cornel West (eds) *Post-Analytic Philosophy*. New York: Columbia University Press, 3–19.

Roobeek, Annemieke J. M. (1987) 'The crisis in Fordism and the rise of a new technological paradigm'. *Futures*, 19 (2): 129–54.

Rustin, Michael (1987) 'Place and time in socialist theory'. *Radical Philosophy*, 47: 30–6.

Schoenberger, Erica (1988) 'From Fordism to flexible accumulation: technology, competitive strategies and international location'. *Society and Space*, 6 (3): 245–62.

Scott, Allen J. (1986) 'Industrialization and urbanization: a geographical agenda'. *Annals of the Association of American Geographers*, 76 (1): 25–37.

Soja, Edward J. (1985) 'Regions in context: spatiality, periodicity, and the historical geography of the regional question'. *Society and Space*, 3 (2): 175–90.

Stephanson, Anders (1987) 'Regarding postmodernism – a conversation with Fredric Jameson'. *Social Text*, 17: 29–54.

Storper, Michael (1987) 'The post-Enlightenment challenge to Marxist urban studies'. *Society and Space*, 5 (4): 418–26.

Storper, Michael and Christopherson, Susan (1987) 'Flexible specialization and regional industrial agglomerations: the case of the U.S. motion picture industry'. *Annals of the Association of American Geographers*, 77 (1): 104–17.

Swyngedouw, Erik A. (1988) 'Capitalism: quo vadis? Reflections on the spatial structure of flexible production and consumption'. Paper presented to the International Conference on Information, Technology and the New Meaning of Space, International Sociological Association, Research Committee 24, Frankfurt, 15–19 May.

Thrift, Nigel (1987) 'The geography of the late twentieth-century class formation'. In Nigel Thrift and Peter Williams (eds) *Class and Space: The Making of Urban Society*. London: Routledge & Kegan Paul, 209–53.

Tydeman, John and Kelm, Ellen Jakes (1986) *New Media in Europe: Satellites, Cable, VCRs and Videotex*. London: McGraw-Hill.

Williams, Raymond (1983) *Towards 2000*. London: Chatto & Windus/Hogarth Press.

Worpole, Ken, Morley, David and Southwood, Russell (1987) *On the Town: A Strategy for Leisure and Choice*. Stevenage: South East Economic Development Strategy.

Young, Robert M. (1988) 'Postmodernism and the subject: pessimism of the will'. Paper presented to the Conference on Rethinking the Subject in Discourse, McGill University, Montreal, March.

EURO POP

I became a rock'n'roll fan through Radio Luxembourg. This wasn't unusual in Britain at the time – the late 1950s – and it's only in retrospect that I realize what a strange musical medium this was. The service was popular with British teenagers both as a source of American music and, we supposed, as an American musical experience in itself – the ads, the sales patter, the clarion call of the new; so very different from the BBC's avuncular condescension. But compared with the harder-to-find American Forces Network there was also something comfortingly provincial about Lux's approach – about the downmarket British ads, the shows in which UK record companies like Decca and Pye pushed bright cover versions of American hits, the way the disc jockeys jollied along their youth community – less a community of consumers, then, than a community of would-be consumers, pushed up against a shop window of American goods that could never quite be ours.

The Luxembourg listening experience was, in short, deeply British (the hardest aspect of our pop sensibility to explain to Americans). Its 'illicitness' was defined against the BBC notion of youth music, and it offered rock'n'roll as a secret that could be devoured under the blankets of a middle-class bedroom (for me Brylcreem and acne cures were every bit as exotic as Elvis Presley himself). I knew my parents had no idea that this music even existed (it was years later that I realized that they had used Radio Luxembourg and Radio Normandie themselves, before the war) but I had no clear sense of why it was, anyway, floating somewhere above the house, available but always liable to fade away, to burst into dangerous volume, to be overlaid with the indistinct gabbling of foreign tongues. (I sometimes wonder if there isn't a generation of British rock fans who still listen to music as if we were overhearing it, taking part in someone else's conversation which might, at any moment, be cut off.) I suppose this was the Americanization of youth culture, the way Richard Hoggart *et al.* agonized at the time, but, as a vicarious experience, it felt like something else: we were somehow sharing the post-war European sense of being occupied.

Thirty years later I'm a Europop fan – hate most rock music – and get my musical kicks not under the sheets with backbeat and doowop men, but in hotel bedrooms during conferences and 'weekend breaks', tuned to satellite and cable services, to MTV Europe and Sky and Super channel, flicking the switch not so much to find a song or image that I like but just to confirm that something odd is still happening out there, as English deejays I've never heard of explain to Dutch and Belgian teenagers what's really hip, and minor British acts turn out to be star guests, judging new releases, chatting to audiences of young Swedes and Spaniards, with a verve they'd never show at home. In these pop services there's a new youth sensibility on display, and the 'pan-European' ads (for Coke and Pepsi, clothes and coffee) and promo videos become a single blur – the same sounds, the same images. This is the Benetton generation, clean, bright-eyed and very, very healthy. These are our masters now, I think, as another group of scrawny, pasty Brits appears on screen, singing for their supper.

Radio Luxembourg lost its mystique, I suppose, with the rise of the pirate radio stations in the mid-1960s. The pirates offered a much more vivid version of commercial broadcasting (most of them were, in effect, American commercial stations) and they flattered us with their attention. But the really important change in British pop sensibility (the reason why the pirates flattered us) was the result of the unprecedented American sales success of the Beatles and British beat. Before then (something conveniently forgotten now) British cover versions of rock'n'roll were as unconvincing as those of any other European country (so that Johnny Halliday was, for example, rather better than Cliff Richard at being Elvis Presley). And British pop fans were certainly less cool, less *hard* than their European peers – the Beatles, after all, learned what live rock'n'roll really meant in Hamburg, and the mod look was rooted in a fantasy of Frenchness, in the allure of the 'discotheque'. The stylishness with which British bands played American music might have been a result of their art school education, but their look was clearly continental – by David Bailey from a film by Jean-Luc Godard, by John Stephens from a street in Rome. What followed, the so-called 'British invasion' of America, marked, rather, the real moment when British pop was 'Americanized', as the USA became British musicians' main object of interest and address, and as US record companies competed for London office space and British blues guitarists. Pop became rock and the ideological distinctions involved (the trivial versus the serious, commerce versus art) were overlayed with a new sense of geography: Britain as a European country versus Britain as, somehow, a musical American state.

This was the moment, the 1970s, when for most British listeners Europop came to mean two equally despised kinds of non-rock music – Eurovision Song contest entries and package-holiday disco. The two forms were, in fact, much the same, resting on a bouncy 4:4 beat, on chirpy singalong choruses, on a Eurospeak which simply strung together all those phrases – voulez-vous; achtung achtung; chirpy chirpy cheep cheep – which are known everywhere. The difference was that Eurovision music was clearly white, with a tendency to an over-emotional flourish in Italian or German ballad style, while the holiday disco drew on a black beat – Afro-American, Afro-Caribbean, African – to conjure up its sense of sunshine, and was, lyrically, deliberately silly – if the high point of the Eurovision Song Contest was the victory of Abba, the ultimate summer holiday group was the Goombay Dance Band.

I liked Abba from the start (it took me longer to get into the Balearic beat) because they took clean white pop to an intensity (or, rather, superficiality) of cleanliness and whiteness that rendered them abstract. As Philip Tagg remarked, Abba were the ultimate Swedish (read European) pop group in their very plasticity; it was because not a single element of their sound was 'naturally' Swedish that they could be heard, in the mid-1970s, as a profoundly Swedish (read European) band. No popular American (or then British) musicians could have been so rootless. And other aspects of Abba's approach presaged other things to come. They were the first group to make music in obvious layers, tracks laid down one upon another, with no sense of spontaneity, no attempt at synchronicity at all; they were the first group to realize the full possibilities of global TV promotion, producing 3-minute clips that could be slotted into every light entertainment show in the world; they were the first group to build a career on the celebration of insincerity – no one ever thought that the love songs they sang had anything to do with their (equally publicized) off-stage lives.

The story goes that when Abba split, Agnetha let it be known that she was looking for someone from the rock world to write and produce her first solo album. Elvis Costello, long an Abba fan, leapt at the opportunity to show his appreciation of this Euroform and sent over a demo tape; Agnetha was appalled – she wanted credibility as a 'real' singer. Her album was eventually produced, predictably, by Phil Collins. Costello was, as usual, too far ahead of the pop game for his own good, because the 1980s saw, indeed, the recuperation of the tackiest aspects of European pop music – its Eurovision and holiday beats – by the hippest operators on the British scene.

The crucial move occurred in gay clubs, when 'high energy' dance music (still, essentially, the speeded-up Motown sound which in the 1970s defined 'Northern Soul') was replaced by Eurobeat, the dance music churned out by mass producers in Germany and Italy to meet the ever-avaricious middle-class disco demand. Eurodisco followed much the same rules as Eurovision and Euro-holiday songs, if with greater rhythmic emphasis; easy, familiar electro-phrases backed an 'expressive' voice. So what was the sudden appeal of this long-familiar formula to Britain's gay clubbers who were, at this time, the most sophisticated of all Britain's regular dancers?

To begin with, Eurodisco appealed less to the dancers themselves than to the deejays and record producers who supplied their sounds. It was cheap to make, resting economically on the fast turnover of product rather than on any sort of starmaking, and it was a form controlled by producers (rather than artists or record companies) which, unlike northern soul, didn't depend on myths of street truth or soul. Because Eurorecords had to have immediate cross-national appeal, musical simplicity was of the essence – a bouncy beat, just one chorus hook, elementary lyrics. The fun of these records was entirely a matter of sound quality, but once a record was a hit it took on a kind of sleazy, nostalgic charm of its own. It was precisely the brazen utility of these records, in short, that gave them gay disco consumer appeal too (while their continued exclusion from the airwaves, from the mainstream of UK pop taste, preserved their cult value). Eurodisco also had an obvious element of camp – British club audiences took delight in the very gap between the grand gestures of Eurosingers (familiar from years of the Eurovision Song Contest) and the vacuity of their songs.

At the time I thought it bizarre and even slightly distasteful that the most mundane and derivative form of European mass music was becoming a British club cult. It was like picking on someone feeble to be one's friend so as always to have someone there to patronize. But within a couple of years (these deejays knew what they were doing) Eurodisco had become the basic soundtrack for mainstream teenage life in Britain too. It is quite apparent now for example (look at the singles charts) that British pop tastes are much more like those in other European countries than like those in North America, and I'm quite sure a young Briton would feel more immediately at home in a European than in an American club, in a European than in an American record store. Such a striking shift in sensibility is best explained through the success stories of the two British groups most obviously dependent on Euro-ideas for their sales, the Pet Shop Boys and Stock, Aitken, Waterman, the production team.

The SAW story is, in some ways, the more straightforward. Pete Waterman himself was schooled in the northern soul, high energy, gay disco world and, as a deejay turned producer, he appreciated the economics of Eurodisco. It suggested a way in which a capital-less hustler could, occasionally, hit pay dirt. What he also understood (as an ex-Mecca deejay, trained to be sensitive to the 'ordinary' youth pop market) was that to move this music from gay club to teen mainstream meant *adapting* it. First, it was necessary to invest Euro-sounds with high production values. Just by using the most sophisticated available recording equipment this cheap music could be made to sound expensive, could be given a sheen (this was the Abba lesson) that would guarantee radio as well as club play. The records had to sound good, that is, even when not being played at full, sweaty volume. Second, for the *Smash Hits*-reading, singles-buying British market it was necessary to provide instantly recognizable faces to go along with the instantly hummable hook-lines. The singers' voices might still be anonymous but their images had to be strong – whether Top Shop girls like Mel and Kim, or a Top Shop boy like Rick Astley. And one brilliant, money-saving scheme SAW came up with was to use stars who already had a clear picture – Samantha Fox, Kylie Minogue from the Australian TV soap *Neighbours*; they didn't need any more expensive image-building.

The Pets' success represents something else – not just the clever adaptation of the camp sensibility of Eurobeat to the British pop formula of two-boy-boffins-with-a-synthesizer, nor just a mastery (derived from true love) of disco pastiche, but also a clearheaded understanding of the exigencies of the European *market*. By the mid-1980s it was clear to British record companies, first, that profits could no longer be realized on best-selling records that were bestsellers in Britain alone, and, second, that, at least in the short term, Europe was a much better target for international sales than the USA; it was nearer, more volatile, quicker to react to the new and the novel (particular if they were British). The rise of video promotion, first exploited with MTV in the USA in mind, also made it possible to reach right across Europe without the need to tour. The travelling circuit, for most British bands now, is made up of TV studios (not clubs or festivals) and miming on the music shows of Germany and Spain, Italy and France, and is now the most crucial (and most hated) aspect of a band's sales work.

If the British recuperation of Eurobeat was the chart story of 1987 (the triumph of Stock, Aitken, Waterman; the consolidation of Pet Shop Boys' success), in 1988 an even more unexpected turnaround occurred. Package holiday pop was recuperated in the guise of 'acid house' Formally the origins of acid house as a dance-floor genre lie in the Chicago house scene (and the name 'acid house' was almost certainly first derived from the local, Chicago slang for sampling – acid burning – rather than having any psychedelic significance). But the resulting experiments with electro-phasing and deep soul vocals, as House producers filled up the ever-expanding holes in their rhythm tracks with ever-more intense noise, had an immediate appeal to the British deejays working the Mediterranean holiday beat. Along the Costa Brava and the streets of Ibiza the usual taste distinctions operating in the British club scene (with a sharp institutional separation between rock and pop, funk and punk, rap and teen beat) were inoperative; everybody, whatever their tastes, had to go to the local holiday disco, and, anyway, in continental Europe such fine distinctions had never really developed on the dance floor – it was still okay, for example, to play Led Zeppelin back to back with the Bee Gees. The challenge for British deejays in this setting was to exploit the confusion of categories, not just seguing from a hard rock to a Euro beat, but also house-style, constructing and deconstructing the genre conventions themselves, setting a sixties guitar solo against an eighties drum programme, using their own play-back and sampling equipment to psychedelicize the simplest beach ditty, to make available the most honoured old rock or soul or jazz tracks for a new sort of collective romp. And when these deejays got back to their London clubs they couldn't see any good reason not to continue to provide these sunny, goofy sounds, to continue to programme roomfuls of waving arms and legs, dancers grinning inanely not so much because of the drugs taken but in memory of the sheer idleness of their holidays. Acid house was, for once, a British youth/music cult that was not in earnest.

The significance of acid house is not that it is in itself a European dance-music form – the music involved is still derived (if increasingly via British sampling engineers) from the dance floor's traditional Afro-American sources – but that it is dance music filtered through a European sensibility. British fans here as elsewhere are having to accept (like British record companies) that in global, quantitative terms they are less significant consumers not just than the Americans or Japanese, but also than the West Germans, than the sales groupings of Scandinavia, the Benelux countries, the Italian/Spanish axis. For visiting American musicians these days London is just a stop between Stockholm and Paris, and accounts of the 'European' market and its appropriate sales images and sounds are no longer necessarily based on British teen taste. The conventions of 'classic' rock, for example, are now determined by a northern European market in which the tastes (and musicians) of Britain are become steadily less important. Hence the success of the German-based 'hard rock and heavy metal magazine', *Metalhammer*, which, founded in 1984, now has pan-European monthly sales of 350,000, with special editions published in France, Spain, Holland, and Scandinavia, as well as in Britain (where sales are relatively small). In its pages any distinction between 'authentic' (Anglo-American) and 'imitation' (European) rock bands would be ludicrous – authenticity is a matter of truth-to-convention, and the conventions of heavy metal are better understood in Germany and Sweden than anywhere else.

But what interests me here is not that continental European producers are just as adept as Britons now in making (and selling) standard rock (Europe) or teenybop (a–ha) or disco (Milli Vanilli) stars, but that the continent is once more (as in pre-Beatle days) providing us with models of pop consumption. The most striking example of this is the least noticed – the rise of 'world music' in general, and African music in particular, as the new measure of authenticity by which 'real' popular-music lovers distinguish themselves from the mindless hordes of Eurodisco dancers. In fact African music, at least, reaches us almost exclusively via France, via French studios, French engineers, and French producers, via, most importantly, French audiences whom the musicians have learnt to please. The appeal of African music in Britain is as much a triumph of French as African pop values, as any glimpse of French pop TV (and the 1988 success of Moray Kante's 'Yeke Yeke') makes clear.

For record companies preparing for 1992 (and it is worth remembering that three of the five majors – Thorn-EMI, Polygram and BMG – are now European controlled) standardization of taste (which is taken for granted) is less of an issue than standardization of copyright laws and licence fees, but all the evidence is that Europe *is* becoming a distinctly important music market. To put it summarily: if, in the 1950s, the 'teenager' (and teenage music) was an American concept, in the 1980s 'youth' (and youth music) have become European.

There are two reasons for this. First, while in the USA record company attention has been shifting demographically, to the grown-up world of compact disc players and 'classic' rock radio formats, in Europe youth has been seen as the vanguard of a new sort of media consumer. The various pan-European satellite and cable services were, until recently, quite clearly youth-used and youth-led. Young people are still the most consistent audience for Sky and Super channels, and youth services like Skytrax and Music Box were crucial in persuading households to subscribe to cable services in the first place. In their exploration of the possibilities of pan-European sales campaigns, advertisers have, thus, had most success with youth-aimed goods – soft drinks, clothes, cosmetics, and music itself. In this context, youth music, pop, is the 'global language' which transnational advertisers must speak, and the traditional image of the young consumer – open to suggestion, forward-looking, hedonistic, impatient – has become essential to the selling of the new media, if only for ideological reasons. To change people's viewing and listening and reading habits, entrepreneurs like Rupert Murdoch rely on the image of the new, sophisticated, media-literate, *young* consumer.

From the music industry's point of view this means that teenagers continue to be a useful market even if their direct economic clout is clearly in decline (as indicated by the falling sales of singles, for example). The TV programmes and films and advertisers who want to reach (and construct) the youth audience *are* still in the market for youth music which also means that, increasingly, Europe is the only significant setting for traditional record-business promotion practices – for expertise in image-making, in packaging, in the creation of new stars. It isn't only in teeny bop and heavy metal that Europe has recently become the source of new faces, even black American dance music now only reaches mainstream white American pop taste *via* the European club scene.

The other reason for the continued resonance of youth and the youth market in Europe is that it is still a significant political category. Here (unlike in the USA) young people are, in part, defined by public policy, and in youth clubs and services, on youth television and radio, 'youth' is still best signified (or attracted) by its music. One consequence is that in many European countries, if only through the devices of a public service 'youth' radio station like BBC Radio 1, rock and teenage pop music continue to be supported and subsidized whatever their actual commercial worth.

But, in the end, what matters about Europop is not its material base but its aesthetic, which does seem to me quite different from rock and roll, the American articulation of pop taste with which we've lived so long. Rock and roll remains rooted (viz Bruce Springsteen and U2, the most America-fixated, tradition-conscious rock acts of our time) in concepts of authenticity, in notions of a fixed code of musical and emotional truths. Europop, whether (in British terms) we're talking Pet Shop Boys, Stock Aitken Waterman or Acid House, rests on both a confusion of musical categories and, more importantly, on a sense of a kind of rootless self-invention (which is why Michael Jackson and Madonna are the most European of American pop stars).

Eurobeat, in short, describes the noise where teen commerce, conceptual art, and the gay scene collide. It's not surprising that these days European stars, not American rockers, have the most important things to say about desire because on the Euroscene there's a thin line between the mainstream and the avant-garde, between bland – Stock, Aitken, Waterman – and startling – Pet Shop Boys – sex. My fantasy, as we approach the 1990s, is to broadcast Radio Luxembourg across the USA so that there, too, they can have the sense that something strange is happening, something they can't quite understand but want – just as we once wanted rock'n'roll.

Strathclyde University,
Glasgow, Scotland

DUNCAN WEBSTER

'WHODUNNIT? AMERICA DID': RAMBO AND POST-HUNGERFORD RHETORIC

O n 19 August 1987 Michael Ryan shot sixteen people in the small town of Hungerford in the south-east of England, and then turned one of his many guns on himself. The event seemed so shocking not just because of the scale of the slaughter and the number of guns legally owned by Ryan, but also due to a feeling that such random shootings were unprecedented in Britain. When Margaret Thatcher visited the town, the day after the massacre, she remarked, 'I feel rather like most people, there are no words in the English language which could adequately describe what happened.' Calling the killings 'an evil crime', she repeated 'We have never had anything like it in this country, and there must be people like me who cannot find the words' (*Guardian*, 21 August 1987: 1). However, a word swiftly filled this gap – Rambo. My analysis centres on the role of the term 'Rambo' in commentaries on the Hungerford massacre, and the possible reasons for its use.

Almost a year after the crimes, in July 1988, the *Sunday Mirror*'s front page announced a story on 'Rambo and the Hungerford backlash'. Under the headline 'No, No, to Rambo', Peter Cliff wrote that by 'a macabre coincidence' *Rambo III* would be released in Britain on the anniversary of the killings, and suggested that Sylvester Stallone's film would 'revive the horror' for Hungerford's residents. The town's former mayor, Ron Tarry, is quoted: 'A lot of people identify Ryan with Rambo. We don't need this film as a reminder.' Ken Hall, 'who came face to face with the real life Rambo during his rampage', comments, 'Surely this film can be held back for a while.' He and his daughter Carol, who received an award for bravery for her aid to Ryan's victims, talk of the lasting effects of the event, and the trauma of the anniversary. She adds, 'The last thing any of us need at this very emotional time is for another Rambo movie to be released.'

The piece continues with comments from the local MP, from a local policeman, from an academic (Professor Timothy Wheeler of the Dorset Institute) who declares that 'Rambo-type films should be banned', and from one of the town's clergymen. Hungerford does not actually have a cinema, but the owners of the nearest one, in Newbury, assure the *Sunday Mirror* that they won't show *Rambo III*. The readers are also reassured by the boss of a local video shop, who says: 'I took Rambo videos off my shelf immediately after the tragedy and I haven't replaced them.' The piece is illustrated by a familiar photograph of Michael Ryan with his wispy beard and jungle hat, captioned 'Killer', a still from *Rambo III* captioned 'Screen Hero', and a photograph of Carol Hall with the caption, 'Heroine' (*Sunday Mirror*, 10 July 1988: 4–5). The juxtaposition of 'Heroine' and 'Screen Hero' produces an opposition of real and false bravery, but the accompanying article denies the possibility of opposing 'real' and 'false' violence, 'Killer' and 'Screen Hero', Ryan's real violence and Stallone's acting. That opposition is not brought into play because, as already quoted, 'A lot of people identify Ryan with Rambo.' The question here is how was that identification so easily and unquestioningly established?

The ubiquitous comparison of Ryan and Rambo draws on a series of ongoing debates about the effects of screen violence, about masculinity, and about the 'Americanization' of Britain in the 1980s. This identification also gives these debates an added centrality and urgency 'after Hungerford'. In the wake of the shootings, a number of positions can be identified: liberal, moral-conservative, populist, feminist. Although various causes were suggested for Ryan's violence, and different meanings were found in the crime, the widely shared use of the Rambo symbol implied more agreement than actually existed. Rambo appears to be the point where these analyses meet, but each position produces the object it deplores, thus creating different Rambos. This article will outline both the agreement and the differences. I am not arguing that this involved any conspiracy, or intentional manipulation of the ensuing 'moral panic', but that the dovetailing of these discourses, and their overlap around the Rambo figure, created some uneasy and unconscious alliances. This gave the Ryan/Rambo identification a self-evident quality, which in turn allowed a tragic crime to lead to an increased policing of the cultural.

The celluloid loner

After the killings both ITV and the BBC cancelled or postponed a number of programmes. Sarah Benton wrote in the *New Statesman* 'In praise of cancelling TV violence'. Michael Ryan is 'dubbed for perpetuity as the Rambo killer':

No one will ever know whether or not Ryan was influenced by TV portrayals of murderous men *but that may not be the point*. Without collusion among newspaper editors, it was a film portrayal of casual male violence which immediately provided the name for Ryan's act. We all understood, where once the Bible for the masses or Greek legend for the elite would have provided the instant imagery. (*New Statesman*, 4 September 1987: 10; my italics)

'*We all understood*': readers of the *Sun* and the *Statesman*, the *Express* and the *Guardian*, are united by Rambo, who has taken the place of the Bible and

Greek legends. In other words, myth. In his preface to *Mythologies*, Roland Barthes speaks of his resentment of the confusion of 'Nature and History', his impatience with the 'naturalness', the '*what-goes-without-saying*', of the myths of daily life. 'Right from the start, the notion of myth seemed to me to explain these examples of the falsely obvious' (1957/73: 11). The theoretical essay that concludes that collection is also relevant: 'every myth can have its history and its geography; each is in fact the sign of the other: a myth ripens because it spreads' (149). Barthes discusses the 'social geography of myths', the papers they move through, their successive waves of media amplification, and so on. In Barthes' terms, Rambo was already a mythical figure *before* the Hungerford shootings; however the social geography of the myth generated different meanings around Rambo, to fit different contexts. Michael Ryan's murders provided the occasion for these differences to be ignored, allowing the myth to cohere. The need to refer to Rambo was shared by very different publications, and Rambo appears across the spectrum of the press, in readers' letters as well as editorials, in Hungerford reporting and in the more analytical pieces in the weekly and monthly political magazines. The repetition testifies to the *overdetermined* nature of the appeal to Rambo, and to the overlapping contexts that made this 'agreement' possible.

A BBC1 *Panorama* documentary on 'Violence on Television', presented by Kate Adie on 15 February 1988, located the mistake that turned into a myth. A witness thought Ryan had been wearing a headband like Rambo's. Kate Adie pointed out that this mistake was inflated by the more inventive reports of violent videos being found at Ryan's house. 'Michael Ryan did not look like Rambo, nor did he dress like Rambo. He probably didn't own a video.' She added that those who knew Ryan said that he hardly ever watched television. On 16 February, BBC1's morning feedback programme, *Open Air*, featured this item with Adrian Milne, its producer, and Kate Adie answering callers' questions and taking part in a studio discussion with a Cardiff panel. Surrounded by reassuring signs of British differences and rituals (items on Welsh tea dances and an announcement of the winners of the Shrove Tuesday pancake-stuffing competition), Adie's factual challenge to the Ryan/Rambo identification provoked a resistance from the Welsh viewers. 'I was quite surprised to find that Michael Ryan *wasn't* dressed as Rambo': this comment was joined by others expressing shock at the lack of evidence connecting violence on screen to violent acts. The mistaken description of the headband is understandable from a shocked witness and from journalists looking for a 'handle' for reporting an unprecedented event. But the difficulty in refuting the mistake, the resistance to the facts, reveals that this mistake, unlike other errors in Hungerford reporting, doubled as a metaphor. To try and establish facts overlooks that, in Sarah Benton's words, 'that may not be the point'. The factual basis for seeing Ryan as Rambo, or as influenced by Rambo, was never as important as 'Rambo', a sign for *male* violence, for *American* violence, and for *Hollywood* violence. These contexts could replace the factual, and in so doing reinforce, rather than contradict, a 'commonsense' view of the effects of screen violence.

The reference to Rambo is hardly ever anchored in analysis of the films. 'Rambo' functions independently of the films in which he is the hero, leaving their narratives for a new discursive career. There had only been two Rambo films made before Ryan's massacre – *First Blood* (1982) and *Rambo: First Blood II* (1985) – but these tend to be conflated into 'Rambo', a cultural symbol for a more substantial threat. Phrases suggest a larger problem than two films: 'another Rambo movie', 'earlier Rambo films', 'the Rambo series', the 'Rambo cult', the 'Rambo phenomenon', 'Rambo-type films'. Rambo could thus be used in a vague way while suggesting specificity, and this combination added to the reasons for the range of appropriations of this reference. The authors of a study of Channel 4 (*Keeping Faith: Channel Four and Its Audience*), David Docherty and David Morrison, challenge assumptions about public concern over television violence. They confront the confusion outlined above: 'the ludicrous situation in which television was held to be responsible for the Hungerford massacre.' The response 'by government and some broadcasters to Hungerford' is analysed as 'a classic example of the conceptual confusion and misplaced guilt about TV.' They mention the way the press jumped on the detail of the headband, but they suggest that this mistake was shaped by existing myths of Rambo.

> Rambo became a metaphor for violence, created in part by the adulation of the character in the popular press. When those who tried to describe the scene in Hungerford High Street sought a word which identified something of which they had no personal experience, some reached for a term to describe violence and chaos: Rambo. Ryan was Rambo, and as Rambo was an audiovisual creation, television was somehow to blame for Hungerford, despite the fact that *Rambo* had not been shown on television. (*Listener*, 11 February 1988: 5)

It was not, however, just the popular press that was involved in this slippage from Ryan to Rambo to television itself as the focus of concern and public debate. And, as an ironic reminder of the persistence of Rambo-as-metaphor, Docherty and Morrison's argument is accompanied by an illustration of a hand on a TV remote control. Buttons are marked 'Violence', 'Sex', 'Racism', 'Murder', 'Hate', and . . . 'Rambo'.

'The killer who brought terror to the historic market town wore Rambo-style army combat gear.' This adjective was the sole mention of Rambo in the *Guardian*'s coverage the day after the killings. Ryan was profiled as 'The loner who loved his guns', 'the quiet man who suddenly lost all control'. Interestingly, there is no mention of film or television, but instead other sources are suggested for Ryan's obsession with firearms: 'He was a marksman, said to have taken part in the Bisley Championships, a former soldier, and dealer in guns.' He had 'reportedly' served with the Parachute Regiment (*Guardian*, 20 August 1987: 1). Many of these details may be as erroneous as the Rambo headband, but it is significant that they were not followed up. No paper carried the headline – 'Para Massacre'.

By the next day, possibly influenced by the tabloids' unanimous choice of Rambo in their coverage, the *Guardian* made Rambo central. Andrew

Veitch wrote about 'the mental path to massacre', speculating about Ryan's background: 'An only child of comparatively elderly parents . . . few friends, apparently no girls, described as a wimp, a failed businessman, a string of jobs, at 27 still living with his mother.' But he also speculated about Ryan's viewing: 'He probably despised Rambo. He would have watched the movies, perhaps he had a collection of Rambo videotapes. But as a gun expert he would have known that *First Blood* was about as realistic as *Blazing Saddles*. He, Michael Ryan, could do better than that.' Leaving aside whether Ryan had seen the films or even owned a video, let alone whether two films could be described as a *collection*, this piece seems inspired by other coverage rather than by the event itself. Now that Ryan is so firmly linked with Rambo, in the papers if not in fact, something must be said about the connection. On the same page, Christopher Reed looked at the United States, with its greater gun ownership and extensive experience of similar crimes. Despite this experience American psychiatrists 'acknowledge the extreme difficulties in spotting potential Rambos in advance'. And the piece continues by maintaining the Rambo reference even as its use is denied: 'The "Rambo syndrome" itself is more a projection of the public, without a firm medical base, experts believe.' Killers 'may use Rambo trappings but psychiatrists believe they have to be violence-prone in the first place' (*Guardian*, 21 August 1987: 17). The 'Rambo syndrome' is set up to be knocked down, but it is described as the *public*'s projection rather than an invention of the newspapers.

Editorials tended to begin with the astonishing fact that Ryan's weapons were legal (he used a Kalashnikov, a carbine, and a Berretta pistol). But the sense that 'something must be done' was carried over from reform of the gun laws to 'Rambo' and screen violence. The *Guardian* began cautiously with the headline 'Glib theories will not ease the suffering', and with a warning about analysing Ryan's mental state 'on what could only have been the basis of scattered and incoherent evidence and local hearsay' (an attitude that had not prevented the paper printing Veitch's analysis quoted above). After discussing Ryan's legal armoury, the editorial turns to 'the issue of the models whom Ryan might have been emulating'.

> On the evidence so far available, it was the age of Rambo, not the age of Roy Jenkins as liberalising, permissive Home Secretary, which seems above all to have shaped him. The connection was explicit. He was dressed in Rambo style, complete with the characteristic headband. Did Ryan feast on such images – with their majestic dispensing of easy death, as if lives counted for nothing – now pumped night after night into people's consciousness on a scale unknown in any other generation? It is not only Madonna, perhaps, who inspires a breed of passionate 'wanter-bees'. (*sic*)

But after that certainty about the explicit connection, a warning: 'we ought, even so, to be careful before drawing sweeping general conclusions from what one man did in his madness on one particular day'. Gun control must be urgently looked at, but 'we should not pretend that we can yet account for, or can ever completely legislate against, that inexplicable mind-exploding spark' which threw Ryan into violence (*Guardian*, 21 August 1987: 12). Indeed, a later editorial, on the tougher gun controls proposed, concluded that 'a Michael Ryan is probably beyond even the most stringent form of licensing' (*Guardian*, 23 September 1987: 14).

Not surprisingly, the *Mail on Sunday* did not suffer from the *Guardian*'s stress on complexity. Its opinion column, headlined 'Pornography of violence that must now end', began with the urgent need for new gun laws. However, it acknowledged that 'things are never quite as simple as they first seem'. New laws can create 'new problems. Ill-thought-out legislation often produces a nasty after-taste.' The next sentence is a classic of post-Hungerford rhetoric: 'Yet there are certain matters which require no thought whatsoever.' At first this refers to Ryan's legal Kalshnikov, but the piece moves swiftly from the gun to its user, ignoring psychology in favour of culture. 'It is clear, however, that something has got to be done about violence on TV and at the cinema. Pornography of violence is as bad as –if not worse than – pornography of sex.'

> Films like Rambo and its offshoot and Death Wish and its follow-ups should simply be refused public exhibition.
>
> They are obscenities and they do great harm. There is not a shred of artistic merit to recommend them. Those who are responsible pollute us all. They are the equivalent of drug peddlers. They dispense a hideous brew of violence and deranged ideology designed to stimulate the weakest and saddest members of our society.
>
> They collect their money and shield their eyes from the consequences of their actions. They take the liberal values in which we as a country take so much pride and then distort them.
>
> It is time their influence on our age was ended for ever. (*Mail on Sunday*, 23 August 1987: 8)

Reforming the law on firearms is more difficult than it first appears, but it now seems that banning films would not create 'new problems', nor leave 'a nasty after-taste'. Although it is interesting to note that the *Mail on Sunday* finds anti-Communism a 'deranged ideology', what is more relevant for this analysis is the combination of vagueness and specificity, 'Films *like* Rambo and its *offshoots*'.

The *Observer*'s editorial, 'Hungerford: the shadow of the gunman', concentrated on the need to control Britain's expanding gun culture. Included in this is a brief discussion of 'the wider cultural issue of Rambo, the celluloid loner pitting his firepower against the world, dispensing "justice" in a spray of bullets.' For most viewers this is 'harmless entertainment'; for some it is 'a benign safety-valve' for aggressive feelings; but for 'a very small few, it is a dangerous macho image to be imitated in real life'. The *Observer* argued that censorship was not the answer (although the BBC was praised for its 'social responsibility' in withdrawing programmes), for a 'more practical' and 'less hazardous' measure would be to prevent easy access to firearms' (*Observer*, 23 August 1987: 8). Roland Butt's contribution to a

BBC seminar on 'Violence and the media', took exception to this 'statistical diminishing', calling it 'wrong and . . . intellectually dishonest. *At Hungerford, one was enough.*' He reverses the *Observer*'s argument that censorship is not as important as gun control: 'The state of mind of the man with a gun seems to me to be more significant than his possession of it' (BBC, 1988: 36; my italics). By this logic one would ban religion because Peter Sutcliffe (the infamous 'Yorkshire Ripper') claimed he had heard the voice of God telling him to kill prostitutes, although this is not a notion considered by Butt, the *Times'* guardian of moral values.

The rhetoric has passed through the looking-glass: Rambo replaces the AK-47 to signify the shock of the event, and then replaces Ryan's psychosis as the *cause* of the event. Rambo is the centre of this writing, not as a *celluloid* loner since even the censorship debate concerns television rather than film, but as a *discursive* construct, a creature of British journalism rather than Hollywood. As the Ryan/Rambo knot was drawn tighter it was enough to assert the connection and declare it obvious. A later *Guardian* editorial began with the certainty of the need for changes to the gun laws, and went on to wonder whether the government would also 'seek to constrain the violence now pumped out night and day on the television screen, in the cinema, and through the video recorder'.

> That Michael Ryan's rampage was strongly influenced by, even in some senses modelled on, the Rambo movies is *not in serious doubt*: both in the way he dressed for his *mission* and in the *locations which he sought*, he was *plainly* attempting to re-enact episodes from 'First Blood'. Whether Ryan knew this film from television, from the cinema, or from video *cannot be proved*; but the *link is unmistakeable.* (my italics)

Perhaps the repetition is an unconscious disavowal of the lack of proof, assertion standing in for evidence, but note how Ryan's acts are no longer seen as 'inexplicable', as in the earlier editorial, but as willed: 'mission', 'locations which he sought'. The editorial continues to say that if this was 'the only evidence', the television companies' post-Hungerford 'truce of a kind on TV violence' might be enough. Academic studies are no help, 'for copious research over the past 20 years has always ended up pointing in conflicting directions'. Complex research may be ignored precisely because it is complex, so we can fall back on 'everyday assessment of human nature'. By the editorial's conclusion, the writer starts to back off, realizing that 'tight central controls' over television, from 'a government which is showing some zest for ordaining what we're permitted to read, would be a dangerous restraint on expression' (*Guardian*, 25 August 1987: 10). However, this is not a liberal opposition to censorship, rather the argument is that something must be done, and because we have an authoritarian government, television had better do it for itself.

Ironically, while the editorial decided to set academic studies aside, Andrew Rawnsley discussed them elsewhere in the same issue, and decided that 'Fog shrouds the truth'. If there is a link between screen violence and violent acts, Rawnsley writes, we do not know how it operates, nor whether consuming violent or pornographic material sublimates or intensifies feelings: 'Jack the Ripper might have settled into private eccentricity if Victorian London had video shops; Michael Ryan might have been just another loser if modern Britain had not had them.' He comments that the power of Mrs Whitehouse's position (as Chair of the National Viewers and Listeners Association) is not her dubious figure of 700 studies, all proving television to be the most important cause of violence, but her appeal to common sense, the same appeal as made in the paper's editorial. For Mary Whitehouse, Rawnsley argues, 'the massacre was an almost exquisite endorsement of the views she has pressed so long and so loudly'. Rawnsley ignores the fact that Hungerford only endorsed her views because the press invented a video-watching, Rambo-crazed killer. He doesn't point this out because he's too busy adding to the construction himself: 'Michael Ryan *plotted* his murders in *almost exact replication* of those of his screen hero in First Blood, shown late at night on BBC-1 last September' (*Guardian*, 25 August 1987: 17, my italics). A crucial word here is 'plotted', which helps explain the power of the Ryan/Rambo identification. Despite the importance of other contexts (feminism, the rhetoric of the British Left), which prepared a 'liberal' paper to consider censorship, another factor behind the certainty about Rambo was a basic need for a filter that would give Ryan's murders some kind of meaning.

How could Ryan be said to have *plotted* his killings? The word introduces the reassurance of a narrative shape, as well as a facile explanation. Rather as the experience of combat differs from the intelligibility of the markers on the maps at headquarters, so these shootings contrast with what the papers saw as their model. 'He was just strolling along the road, shooting at anything that moved', said a witness, and I don't think that '*anything*' is a mistake. 'Anyone' suggests motives, feelings, choices. People who saw him describe psychosis, a withdrawal from reality: 'He was just living in a world of fantasy'. Living *in*, not living out fantasy, smiling while he fired at random. Ryan began his killings by shooting a woman, picnicking with her children in Savernake forest, thirteen times in the back. Ryan drove back to Hungerford, stopping at a garage and shooting at the cashier. His next act was to set fire to his house; returning to his car he found that it wouldn't start, so he riddled it with bullets. He killed his dog and later asked a policeman to see that it got a decent burial. Because his mother wasn't there, because his car wouldn't start, he began shooting at neighbours, the police who arrived at the scene, and at anyone he saw on his way to the High Street. He had killed seven people by the time he shot his mother four times, twice at close range. Later he would ask a policeman how she was, fourteen times. The killings were random, with the victims unable to understand what was happening: one neighbour, Mrs Dorothy Smith, aged 77 and partially deaf, went out into the street on hearing his gunfire, and shouted, 'You stupid bugger. Stop it – you are frightening people to death.' Another pensioner, Mrs Betty Tolladay, who survived being shot by Ryan, heard the bangs while gardening and thought someone was playing with fireworks. She asked Ryan to 'kindly stop that racket'. The killings stopped because, for some reason, Ryan stopped shooting. He walked to his old school where he was finally located and surrounded by police. Talking to the police Ryan described his day as 'like a bad dream', and, referring to his mother, 'I didn't mean to kill her. It was a mistake.' When Sergeant Brightwell replied 'I understand that', Ryan said, 'How can you understand? I wish I had stayed in bed.' He worried about children finding the gun he had discarded earlier. He finally shot himself after saying, 'It's funny, I had killed all those people but I haven't the guts to blow my own brains out.'[1]

'Rambo' makes these actions seem less arbitrary, turning them into a plotted re-enactment. Ryan's killings were supposed to parallel *First Blood* through their locations (both Ryan and Stallone move from a wood to a town) but there is a crucial difference around precisely the meaning of place and home. Ryan drives from a local wood to a local garage, goes home, sets fire to his house, shoots at his neighbours, kills his mother, shoots anyone he sees in the High Street, and walks to his old school, a place not just of education but also of the forming of identity, the training in the norms of masculinity. An attack on home, neighbourhood, family, the places and people of his life is followed by a literal wiping out of his life, his schoolroom suicide. *First Blood* concerns a different but equally problematic idea of home, focused on the problem of the Vietnam veteran's return to the United States. Rambo arrives at a small town only to be mistaken for a hippy drifter rather than a Special Forces veteran. He is run out of town by the chief of police, and when he returns, in protest at his petty harassment, he is arrested. Jail reawakens traumatic memories of Vietnam and Rambo escapes, to be hunted by first the police then the National Guard. The film concludes with explosions and histrionics, but it does raise questions about the scapegoating of the veterans, and the boomerang effect of violence. In David Morrell's original novel, Colonel Trautman, Rambo's ex-commanding officer, says: 'We forced him into it over there, and now he's bringing it all back home' (1973: 164). And the film's director, Ted Kotcheff, talked of Rambo as a Frankenstein's monster created by the army for Vietnam, and then coming home. In fact, Rambo's training overrides his trauma and he uses his reflexes to confuse and evade his pursuers, trying to warn them off rather than to kill them. He surrenders to Trautman at the end of *First Blood*, and *Rambo* begins with him being offered a pardon if he will go on a mission to Vietnam to check on the existence of American POWs still being held. The problem raised by the figure of the veteran is thus displaced onto the mythical American prisoners. There is no longer a questioning of the relation between state and private violence, although the awkwardness of the subtitle – *First Blood II* – retains traces of this problem, in its combination of 'firstness' and repetition. Violence and Rambo are sent back where they 'belong' – in Vietnam not in America's heartland. Thus: 'What you call hell, he calls home', a remark that attempts to close the questions about coming home raised in the first film.

The proposed parallel between *First Blood* and Hungerford overlooks the different situation of the insider and the outsider. Rambo shows up in town and is arrested by the local police; the Thames Valley police processed

Ryan's firearms certificate in fifteen days, although it normally took from two to six weeks to investigate an application. The difference between Ryan and Rambo helps to deconstruct the opposition, common to almost all reports, between the violence and its setting, the quiet, English market town. For Ryan's armoury was built up so easily, not because of the 'Americanization' of Britain as so many reports suggested, but because of the very 'Englishness' of the setting, the country values of shooting and hunting. Julie Burchill discussed the media's insistence that it 'should not have happened here', commenting that 'A great deal of fuss was made about the *smallness* of the town, the *closeness* of the community.' She focused on a certain English smugness about such places, citing A. N. Wilson's comment on the unsuitability of Hungerford for such a crime: 'this little town where you could easily picture Miss Marple riding her bike along the high street. But, of course, Miss Marple was all about murder, and murder in little towns at that.' She detected an unspoken racism behind the assumption that the small town is somehow more essentially English than the multi-racial city: 'imagine the reaction if an Afro-Carribean swanked into Brixton police station and made inquiries about how to get hold of a licence for a Kalashnikov automatic!' (*New Society*, 4 September 1987: 25). The weight of positive values given by our culture to the countryside prevents us seeing that for Ryan the wood was the site of fantasy, not the cinema, and his solitary activity was not watching videos but going shooting or walking the dog. Although Burchill can see this, and can challenge the city/country opposition, she cannot extend this analysis of Englishness by challenging the discourse of 'Americanization'. She is prevented from doing this by her own extreme anti-Americanism, and her other contribution to the Hungerford discussion provides the title for this article: 'Whodunnit? America did'. I will conclude (see below) with a discussion of debates surrounding this issue, but the next section will address the other discourses that helped to produce the 'Rambo' rhetoric.

Is your neighbour a raving Rambo? The moral panic over television

As mentioned above, in the wake of the shootings the television companies withdrew several programmes and postponed others, and the BBC hastened to say that they were not planning to rescreen *First Blood*. Although broadcasters explained this action as informed by sensitivity to public feelings, it was greeted by Mary Whitehouse and others as an admission that programmes were too violent, and that they had direct effects on viewers. Post-Hungerford rhetoric is not just the cries of editors and politicians that 'something must be done'. It is also the rhetoric of 'post-Hungerford' itself, the discussion of the event as a turning point for the policy of the media. Rosalind Coward noted that 'Undoubtedly the activities of a self-styled *Rambo*, Michael Ryan, in Hungerford have accelerated the Tories' desire to "do something" about the question of violence' (1987: 24). 'The horror of Hungerford . . . has put television violence high on the autumn agenda. . . .

No one, especially after Hungerford, should deny real and valid public concern in these areas' (*Guardian*, 21 September 1987: 12). Why did television collude in this process?

Five days after the shootings, Michael Grade, then of the BBC, proposed talks with ITV and Channel 4 on 'long-term measures to deal with screen violence in the wake of the Hungerford massacre' (*Guardian*, 25 August 1987: 26). If this was an attempt to look properly self-restraining, and thus head off government intervention, it failed. Douglas Hurd, the Home Secretary, announced that he had called a meeting with Lord Thomson, chairman of the IBA, and Marmaduke Hussey, chairman of the BBC, to discuss programme standards and portrayals of sex and violence, 'particularly following events at Hungerford' (*Guardian*, 17 September 1987: 2). Sarah Benton asked if it was right 'for TV bosses to appear to claim some responsibility for television in particular, for such apparently non-sensical acts of violence'. It was not 'heavily regulated and controlled TV that brought us Rambo but the free markets of film and newspapers'. Benton also looked at the way journalism reinterprets television: 'It is the popular press, acting in relation to TV, not TV on its own, which has made *Dallas*, *Dynasty* and the *A Team*, let alone Rambo and the *Sun*, into a common language for naming strange forms of life; the stuff of our fantasies, not of our experience' (*New Statesman*, 4 September 1987: 10). Writing in the *National Student* magazine, Alistair McKay compared the title of the 1987 Edinburgh TV festival – 'Television Fights Back' – with Hurd's post-Hungerford summons. He asked 'why no Downing Street summons for the tabloid editors, whose treatment of Hungerford itself ("Maniac Rambo was my Gay Lover" – *The Sun*) might be seen to more directly fuel psychopathic fantasies in the weak minded?' (*NSM* 6, May 1988: 15). The point that the Ryan/Rambo identification belonged to journalism, not fact, is obscured by this attempt to pass the scapegoat, to substitute one simplistic cause for another. What should also be challenged is the reductive search for *one* cause. Colin MacCabe identified both this need and the reason why television was identified as the culprit in this moral panic: 'There must be one simple explanation for Hungerford and television is the best visible example of the new semiotic world in which we live' (1988: 29).

A possible reason for the BBC's and ITV's response to Hungerford, with all the overtones of guilt involved, was to display its self-regulation and social responsibility, and to signal its difference from the world of satellite broadcasting. The *Panorama* on 'Violence on Television', for example, ended with a warning that if television showed less violent material, satellites might fill the gap. And, in McKay's article, Philip Whitehead, ex-Labour MP, now producer, contributed to this 'watch the skies' paranoia with a warning that with satellites: 'Rambo would certainly stalk the skies' (*NSM* 6, May 1988: 17). In this light, it is possible to see the cancellation of programmes as a strategy to highlight the contradiction between the Conservatives' belief in economic deregulation and moral regulation, the BBC and ITV pointing out their restraint with a subtext concerning the possible results of an 'open skies policy'. Again, this can't be said to have been successful. At a Downing Street meeting on the future of broadcasting, Michael Grade warned of a future of satellites bringing pornography, and Mrs Thatcher is reported to have replied, 'that having King Lear's eyes being gouged out on a television set six feet away was also a problem' (*Guardian*, 22 September 1987: 34), a remark that shows that her knowledge of Shakespeare is on a level with her knowledge of Stallone.

But the real context for television's awkward response to Hungerford is the attacks from the government and the press throughout the 1980s, on moral, political, and economic fronts. Television is somehow responsible for rising violence; it is unpatriotic and biased against the government; and it is 'the last bastion of restrictive trade union practices' in Thatcher's phrase. Legal moves around the topic of screen violence include the 'video nasties' panic and the subsequent Video Recordings Act of 1984, Winston Churchill's 1986 proposal to tighten up the obscenity law and extend it to television, and Gerald Howarth's introduction in 1987 of an Obscene Publications Bill, which would have included television and depended on the problematic concept of 'a reasonable person', making the 'offensive' not that which deprives and corrupts but that which offends 'commonsense' notions of acceptable violence and sexuality (Coward, 1987: 25). There is also the Broadcasting Standards Council, whose creation was announced at the Conservative Party Conference in October 1987, following the 1987 election manifesto reference to the 'deep public concern over the display of sex and violence on television', with Lord William Rees-Mogg announced as its chairman in May 1988.

Although there were many questions unanswered about the BSC's relation to other regulating bodies (The Broadcasting Complaints Commission, the BBC governors, the IBA, the Cable Authority), and unease about the extent of its powers, its birthpangs were greatly eased by the unanimity generated by post-Hungerford rhetoric. The moral-conservative position shared by campaigners such as Mary Whitehouse and by the Conservative government is concerned not only to censor images of sex and violence but to promote an image of the family. Hence the focus on television and video: interventions around television or horror videos create the family as an object of concern but also re-establish it as a cultural norm.[2] It is reported that all but one of the Tory MPs who answered a Children's Legal Centre questionnaire 'believed parents have the right to beat their children without being accountable to the state' (*Guardian*, 23 May 1988: 38). In the moral-conservative world view, the state should not intervene to regulate violence in the family but should intervene to regulate television viewing. In a wish to be seen as the true 'party of the family' Labour has made only rare challenges to this move towards tighter forms of cultural policing of television. Indeed, after Hungerford, Labour called for a new government study on possible connections between screen violence and violence in society. When Frank Dobson, Labour's campaign co-ordinator, announced that if 'a possible link is established effective action can and obviously must be taken', he may have been trying to reappropriate the moral ground from the Tories, but he certainly eased the way for Rees-Mogg and the BSC. As did the response of liberal papers such as the *Guardian*, the liberal response to Hungerford being a combination of unease about censorship and anxiety about violent films, with the latter tending to predominate. Or, as Eric Paice's letter put it, 'It is time we woolly liberals came out of the closet on this issue' (*Guardian*, 27 August 1987: 12).

The populist position is as ambivalent as the liberal, with the tabloids veering between a defence of cultural products as 'harmless fun' and a 'law and order' populism demanding the policing of culture. Examples of these two positions can be seen in the papers' mockery of feminist objections to 'Page 3 girls', and the papers' role in the 'video nasties' debate. Interestingly, Rambo received both treatments. In 1985 the *Mirror* organized a Rambo-lookalike contest; in 1988, as we have seen, the *Sunday Mirror* declared 'No, No to Rambo'. In August 1985 the *Sun* screamed 'Rambo Keep Out!', following the plea of the head of the British Safety Council, James Tye, for the film to be censored ('No civilised society can any longer permit the exploitation of the psychos in our midst'). The paper followed that statement by offering 11,000 free preview tickets for the film. Nigel Pollitt reports these details in a discussion of the global success of *Rambo: First Blood II*, and the range of products that helped to transform the film into a wider phenomenon. Not just the book of the film but the T-shirts, the 'Rambograms', the computer game – 'You are Rambo. You are trying to escape from the enemy . . .' (*City Limits*, 30 August 1985: 11–12). One could add the cartoons, the puns, the impersonations, the compound adjectives ('Rambo-style', 'Rambo-like', etc.), even the verbs (to 'do a Rambo', someone 'went Rambo', etc.). Bruce Springsteen becomes 'the Rambo of Rock'; cricket offers 'Rambotham'; put Samantha Fox in the appropriate pose and she becomes 'Sambo'. Rambo represents an excess that can be portrayed, in this populist response, as *funny* (hence the cartoons, and Steve Wright's Radio 1 Rambo impersonator), or threatening, according to context, and with no fixed positive or negative connotations. Hungerford and the tabloids' agreement on the Ryan/Rambo link provided the most powerful context, and allowed a crossover between populist usages of Rambo and other positions on screen violence.

I have analysed in detail the way that Rambo was used as 'rhetorical punctuation' in Left-liberal responses to the US bombing of Libya in 1986 (1988: 231–45). If the *Sun*, as an example of the populist perspective, used Rambo to describe individuals ('Is your neighbour a raving Rambo?'), the Left has most commonly used Rambo as a kind of cultural shorthand for America's interventions in the Middle East and Central America. As part of this position a parallel is suggested between a cinema of reactionary macho heroes and Reagan's foreign policy: the United States is seen as self-conscious about its 'powerlessness' after Vietnam and the Iranian hostages crisis, while conventional notions of masculinity are shaken by the women's movement and gay politics. An action such as Reagan's invasion of Grenada or a film such as *Rambo* are seen as parallel 'resolutions' and revisions of this historical challenge to American power. My argument against this type of analysis is that it overlooks the complexity of reception and genre, seeing

Rambo as a kind of 'ideology-gram' unproblematically delivering a single message. Yet *Rambo* reworks genre as much as it revises history, working as a kind of meta-action movie, mobilizing signifiers of action across genres. Rambo is both John Wayne and Apache Indian; he's James Dean the inarticulate teenager and he's Frankenstein's monster; he's Tarzan and the Incredible Hulk; the Russians and Vietnamese are also Nazis and 'Japs'. He is crucially *double*: the outsider-rebel and the military killing machine, both betrayed by the US government and its secret weapon. These allow audiences to read the discarded figure of Rambo from generational or socio-cultural perspectives which do not centre on Vietnam.

The further danger is that the symptomatic analysis of films can come to replace political analysis. It is clear that the military, the State Department, the CIA, academics, and rightwing think tanks have been more central to the formation of post-Vietnam American policy than have Stallone or Chuck Norris, but you would sometimes doubt this from British coverage of American politics. Many British writers seem unable to resist analysing American foreign policy by looking at Hollywood rather than Harvard, partly because of the strong grip that conservative cultural criticism has on the British Left's anxiety about Americanization. The influence of feminism on Left cultural analysis can be seen in references to Stallone's muscles and his 'phallic' weaponry, but again Rambo is a more complex figure than these suggest. Barbara Creed sees Stallone and Arnold Schwarzenegger as '"performing the masculine". Both actors often resemble an anthropomorphised phallus, a phallus with muscles, if you like' (1987: 65). Embodying masculinity as masquerade or caricature differentiates Stallone from John Wayne, as very self-consciously an object of the gaze as well as a subject of action. Stallone's poses combine contradictory masculine iconography; one minute he's Christ, the next a muscle magazine pin-up. But the complexity of Rambo as an icon of masculinity was overlooked in feminist contributions to post-Hungerford analysis.

Sarah Benton expressed relief at violent programmes being cancelled, welcoming a break from being 'a passive participant in a certain sort of male violence', and adding that it is 'less the sweaty men flourishing gleaming guns and axes that I mind (for they can seem absurd) than the endless loop of women screaming in horror as their nemesis advances' (*New Statesman*, 4 September 1987: 10). Her objection is not to screen violence in itself, but to the exploitation of her fear of male violence. The reference would seem to be to horror movies and it does not appear very relevant to the Rambo debate, more like a leftover from 1984's 'video nasties' panic. This may seem a small point, but the importance of genre has been stressed by feminist criticism itself. One could argue that there is now a gulf between feminist readings of past forms and genres and feminist reactions to present ones: thus the Gothic is viewed as a literary form with the potential to open up tensions within the social construction of femininity (see Modleski, 1984), while Horror is simply violence against women. Feminism's importance in post-Hungerford rhetoric is partly the influence that feminist arguments about pornography and screen violence have had on Left-liberal cultural politics. I will discuss

Rosalind Coward's contributions to the Ryan/Rambo debate in some detail as her argument illustrates the strength of the feminists' position on screen violence (its difference from the moral-conservative arguments and from academic studies of screen violence), but it is also representative in its tension between a sophisticated analysis and a retreat into 'common sense'.

Coward's first reaction begins with the popular press's headlines about Ryan 'running amok in Hungerford, dressed in US military uniform and Rambo-style headband': the *Star*, 'Rambo Killing Field', the *Express*, 'Massacre Rambo kills himself', and the *Sun*, '15 dead and so is mad Rambo'. Coward seems to agree with the tabloids that Ryan took 'a ready-made violent fantasy' and then acted it out. It does not seem to occur to her that the *Sun* is an odd place for a feminist critic to gather her 'facts'. The piece moves from the simplistic model of re-enactment to more complex psychoanalytical notions of fantasy, only to embrace simplicity again as it turns to the rigidly gendered world of recent children's programmes, *Masters of the Universe* and *My Little Pony*. The hardening of gender stereotypes in children's television is seen as somehow 'causing' the popularity of shooting and war games, and helping to explain Michael Ryan (*Guardian*, 1 September 1987: 20). But Ryan grew up with *Blue Peter* rather than *Masters of the Universe*, and there seems something opportunistic in adding Ryan and Hungerford to a discussion of children's programming.

This material, together with its problems, is carried over to a longer article on Hungerford and screen violence in *Marxism Today*. There Coward criticizes the Left for the inadequacy of its response to the violence debate: 'Faced with a number of truly horrific "mass murders", which do indeed seem to derive their style, if not their motivation, from violent cult movies' (neither the crimes nor the movies are named), 'there is a general unwillingness to engage very seriously with the debate about violence and with what the Tories are currently proposing' (1987: 25). Coward stresses that the feminist objection is not to 'violence in the abstract' but to the ways that it is seen as 'a natural part of masculinity in a highly gendered universe'. Against the studies of television violence as a 'fixed and measurable category', she argues for an analysis of 'the dominant *meanings* which surround the portrayal of violence', and the way those meanings are linked to gender (26–7). Again there is an uncertainty of tone, as Coward discusses children's television, violent films, pornography, and hesitates between sophisticated and simplistic accounts of fantasy and effects. There seem to be three main problems with Coward's argument. The first is a tendency to reproduce what she deplores, a rigidly gendered world where male fantasies and cultural forms are totally separated from women's, a tendency which overlooks the complexity of the links between gender and genre, and the negotiations of consumption.

In *Female Desire*, Coward asserts: 'Women don't seem to like the same kinds of fantasies as men. War films, "chaps-against-the-elements" stories, or violent thrillers are all received as completely uninteresting to most women. We just don't find them pleasurable.' She analyses these fantasies, including car chases ('which leave the average woman cold'), in terms of a concern with castration. 'It is really interesting', she writes, 'to see how women react to male fantasies. On the whole we switch off, get on with the ironing while the chaps race over the roof tops' (1984: 202–3). In an admirable attempt to popularize difficult ideas, she sinks here into a reductive approach and a bogus universality. 'Women don't . . .', 'most women', 'we', 'the average woman', 'how women react', 'we . . . *get on with the ironing*': are these the terms with which to challenge essentialism?

Another problem with Coward's argument is suggested by the restricted range of her examples. It is certainly important to link the meanings of screen violence to models of gender, but there is a temptation to single out one form or genre, even a single work, as the privileged site for the cultural construction of masculinity (horror movies, video nasties, Rambo, pornography, children's TV). However, that construction must be seen as working, in contradictory ways, across a range of forms, genres, discourses and institutions, and in television terms, working across cartoons, drama, thrillers, nature documentaries, the news, and so on. With Ryan, for example, the newspapers created a model of masculinity rather like the 'before-and-after' adverts for Charles Atlas muscle-building courses. He was seen as the wimp who turned into Rambo, and attention must be paid not just to Rambo but to the cultural construction of the 'wimp', and the implied norms of masculinity, which are neither wimp nor Rambo. The *Sun*, for example, added up the elements quickly enough (no girlfriend, lived with his mother), and decided he was gay. Masculinity is not just differentiated from femininity, it also works to distinguish itself from effeminacy and weakness. After Hungerford, the BBC cancelled the thriller *Black Christmas* and replaced it with Dick Emery's comedy show. Masculinity is worked on, struggled over, as much in the latter's caricatures of gays as in the film's portrayal of a psycho.

This leads to the third problem, that singling out one form, genre, or film eases a shift from analysis to scapegoating and censorship. Rosalind Coward's expression of the hope that the 'commission on broadcasting' proposed by Douglas Hurd might 'open up a space' for the feminist analysis of screen violence, and might lead to broadcasters being more accountable to the public (1987: 27), might itself be argued to be overoptimistic. Feminist discourse was not listened to post-Hungerford but rather was co-opted by a moral-conservative anxiety about standards, hence the *Mail on Sunday*'s 'pornography of violence'. The result was not a more accountable media, but Rees-Mogg and the BSC. The comparison that should cause feminists, socialists, and liberal participants in the panic over Ryan and Rambo to reflect on their rhetoric, is the notorious Section 28 of the Local Government Act, banning the 'promotion' of homosexuality. There are many shared elements: the taking up of mistaken stories from the tabloids, the concern for children at risk, the simplistic notions of causality (of violence, of sexual identity). It is more difficult to challenge the absurd claims that a 14-year-old boy will 'turn gay' after watching a Derek Jarman film, when it is argued that he will turn psychotic at the drop of a video.

Whodunnit? America did

Colin MacCabe argued that 'the attempts to arraign television for the tragedy at Hungerford' were trying to reproduce a lost, unified national culture (1988: 29). Ryan was so firmly linked to Rambo through the attempt to define this 'national culture' against Americanization. In the *Panorama* analysis of television violence, over a shot of ducks on the river, a picture of quiet Englishness, Kate Adie suggested that after the shock of Ryan's murders in such a peaceful English town, it seemed more relevant to ask about the effects of violent films. Rambo here is an icon of Americanness: since the violence seemed American – the loner with the gun collection – it seemed natural to think of it as *imported*, along with imported violent representations. Adie pointed out that 'a third of all violence on British television comes from America'. An odd argument emerged where violence was seen as natural on American screens and streets: 'But what is so acceptable and unremarkable on American screens is exported to Britain, where it has little connection to daily life'. This simplistic notion of 'reflection' assumes that most Americans live in the life of *Miami Vice* and *Hill Street Blues*, and it was a view which was developed by the journalist Paul Johnson's frequent contributions. Johnson progressed from saying 'America is an extremely violent country' to demanding qualitative and quantitative controls on US television imports: 'I think that anything that comes from America has to be watched very, very carefully indeed, and far too much of it does appear on British screens.'

Next to the demand for an end to the 'pornography of violence', the *Mail on Sunday* printed another cry from the heart: 'Save our vanishing English gardens'. Robin Page lamented the loss of the real English garden with hollyhocks, sweet williams, 'marrows by the compost heap', bees humming, wrens singing, rambling roses, and 'a child making daisy chains to the sound of laughter' (*Mail on Sunday*, 23 August 1987: 8). An accidental juxtaposition no doubt, but a significant one. In the same issue, Julie Burchill used Hungerford for her usual anti-Americanism. Hungerford exposed how 'grotesque habits pass for "normal" in this country, and all countries in the American-speaking world', referring to Ryan's gun collection. We have seen that Burchill argued elsewhere that Ryan could be seen in terms of an English cult of the country, but here America is to blame. However, 'you can blame American influence, as even right-wing Yankophiles are doing now – but you can't blame America for trying. It didn't tie us down and force itself upon us.' Instead, she argues, British governments since World War II have acted as a sort of fifth column, turning 'this sovereign state' into 'the image of an American colony – a cooler Puerto Rico, a more ornate Alaska.' Whenever America 'has been invited to put its sticky, ketchup-stained fingers', these massacres happen. They don't happen in the countries 'in which the Russians interfere', for the psychosis 'of the gunman is the selfishness that fuels capitalism, taken to breaking point.' By now, she appears to have forgotten her point about the British role in Americanization, arguing that we should have 'put up a fight against the groping hand of America'. We need not just tighter gun laws but 'a British fundamentalist revolution, with Enoch Powell as the Ayatollah and Mr Livingstone as Speaker Rafsanjani' (*Mail on Sunday*, 23 August 1987: 18).

Another mullah of British fundamentalism echoed Burchill's answer to the post-Hungerford whodunnit: Jeremy Seabrook writing on 'The horror of Hungerford'. He picked up on Thatcher's claim that this was something 'unknown in this country': 'for such phenomena are certainly not unknown in the United States, that source and model of an enterprise culture which she is so anxious for Britain to emulate'. He lists such American products as 'the promotion of militaristic fantasies, cults of heroes, machismo and survivalism, a vast sex and violence industry that masquerades as entertainment, a worship of fame, respect for "the power of the gun"'; and, of course, mass murders' (*New Society*, 28 August 1987: 15–16). It was not exactly a surprise that Seabrook detected the 'groping hand of America' behind the massacre, since he seems to hold the United States responsible for Thatcherism. The present is a foreign country; they do things differently here. This can be seen in Seabrook's response to the 1988 Budget. He writes of the 'destruction of traditional British values', but also describes these values as 'cheery myths' and 'the self-flattering qualities which the British attribute to themselves . . . tolerance, decency and good humour . . . a love of fair play and justice, and sympathy for the underdog.' Modern Britain is 'an alien imposition on older, more familiar characteristics which we once thought so endearing and ineradicable'. A look at the terms – values, myths, self-flattering qualities, familiar characteristics – shows that even Seabrook cannot quite believe in this vision. He needs it, however, as for him Thatcherism cannot be seen as a product of a *British* crisis: 'The process is akin to that of being colonised, forcibly subjected to external constraints and alien values. If we do not recognize it, perhaps this is because we had grown accustomed to being the initiators of such conquests.' As with Burchill, a recognition that Americanization is a British dynamic is buried by the analogy with colonization. The Empire, which no doubt we ruled with a judicious blend of 'cheery myths' and 'sympathy for the underdog', is at the core of this rhetoric. Unable to be post-imperial, 'we' must be colonized. Seabrook sees Britain's future 'in the crueller, if more rugged social landscapes of the United States', but only because he seems unable to see Britain's past (*Guardian*, 21 March 1988: 34). Seabrook's vanished Britain belongs with the *Mail on Sunday*'s lost hollyhocks, but to describe what has happened to this mythical landscape he talks of 'alien values', a phrase that might be borrowed from a National Front pamphlet.

Hungerford brought out a disavowal and displacement, which reworked Britain into a southern, English pastoral disrupted by Ryan's 'American' violence. The extent of this disavowal is extraordinary, as seen in Chris Reed's coverage of the Las Vegas convention of *Soldier of Fortune* magazine: 'Although military pursuits, gun collections, and macabre fascination with violent death appear as particularly American phenomena, the tragedy of Hungerford has alerted Britain to the (*sic*) presence in our midst. British military activities and especially the SAS are much admired by American combat cultists' (*Guardian*, 31 August 1987: 11). It is surely, though, only in the wave of post-Hungerford illusion that we could be asked to see military pursuits as particularly American. The SAS, for example, have been slavishly admired by the British popular press since the Iranian embassy siege of 1980. It was not American combat cultists who printed 'SAS RUB OUT IRA RATS' but the *Star* (31 August 1988). Another *Guardian* writer, discussing the Pope's visit to America, especially the 'jarring images' of the Pope shaking hands with Clint Eastwood, reflected on the morality of Hollywood. Alex Brummer commented: 'No one in Britain, for instance, needs to be reminded of the destructive influence of Sylvester Stallone's Rambo on a country once renowned for its non-violence (*Guardian*, 21 September 1987: 23). '*No one in Britain*', the Rambo/Ryan link is now such a secure myth that it needs no explanation. But where is this country 'once renowned for its non-violence'? A crime-free country with no riots, no military presence in Northern Ireland, indeed no militaristic culture, no racism, and so on. This innocent England is not just devoid of violence but also of *history*; it resembles the deluded world of 'Ukania' attacked by Tom Nairn (1988). 'Americanization' blocks any analysis of a specifically English crisis. However, 1988 provided a more revealing image of our confused identity and relation to history than Rambo: young English men supporting the English football team in Dusseldorf, singing the national anthem while giving Nazi salutes.

There was a concern with rights, with the liberties of the subject, after Hungerford, but those of the gun-owning subject rather than the television viewer. The coroner at the inquest remarked, 'If you take away the right to bear firearms, you are interfering with people's liberty' (*Guardian*, 30 September 1987: 1). Something had to be done, but obvious measures, such as holding a public inquiry into firearms licensing, were ignored in favour of hysteria about Rambo. Firearms were discussed in a discourse of rights, freedom, balance, and so on, but by and large television was not. David Docherty and David Morrison argue that viewers should not be treated as a passive audience but as *citizens*, forming judgements and making choices (*Listener*, 11 February 1988: 4). Rambo conjured up a number of fears (screen violence, male fantasies and violence, Americanization), but in the end, the key issue became how best to 'protect' a mythical, unified national culture from the external forces of disruption. My final point concerns the *narrowness* of this national culture, which can be seen in the figure chosen to save the country from all that Rambo was seen to represent – Lord Rees-Mogg. A Somerset landowner and ex-Tory candidate, Rees-Mogg has edited *The Times*, headed the Arts Council, and been vice-chairman of the BBC. In that last role, he played a central part in banning the *Real Lives* programme about Northern Ireland, which provoked a journalists' strike. He has also attacked 'advocacy journalism' and denounced BBC drama as 'a public scandal', singling out for criticism a play that, as it turned out, he had not seen.

If Rees-Mogg does not make clear enough the links between how we are governed and how television is regulated, there is a more recent reminder that we are subjects rather than citizens. In September 1988, when Prince Charles opened the Museum of the Moving Image in London, he diverted from his prepared speech to complain about 'the incessant menu of utterly gratuitous violence on both cinema and television – especially television – and most particularly video.' Parents, worried about their children's 'diet of freely available and insensate violence', are told, according to the Prince, the 'palpable nonsense' that there is no direct effect. Once again academic studies are set aside: 'It is high time that someone told these self-appointed experts that they are like the Emperor's set of new clothes – that they are not wearing anything at all' (*Guardian*, 16 September 1988: 1). It is not that existing research contains all the answers (see for example Coward's powerful criticisms of its model of violence). The question here is one of the wilful rejection of the complexity of the issues at stake: which are reduced to the terms of a simple dichotomy: on the one side, children at risk; on the other, ivory tower academics. Mary Whitehouse felt 'immeasurable grati-tude', the Prime Minister was said to have agreed, Rees-Mogg was heartened, and Home Secretary Douglas Hurd gave a speech about television's 'designer violence'. And Rupert Murdoch's *Today* newspaper hailed 'the People's Prince'.

Trent Polytechnic, Nottingham, England

Notes

1 The information here is taken from reports of the inquest (see *Guardian*, 26 September 1987: 3; 30 September 1987: 1–2), and from the television recon-struction, *This Week Special*: 'Hungerford – The Lessons', with John Taylor as the reporter and Christopher Oxley the producer (ITV, 7 January 1988).
2 See Martin Barker's excellent book on the 1950s campaign against horror comics, and the collection edited by him about a modern parallel, the 'video nasties' debate (1984a, 1984b). The ramifications of the 1984 Video Recordings Act are explored in two articles by Julian Petley: *New Statesman*, 8 April 1988: 8; *Independent*, 18 August 1988: 11.

References

Barker, Martin (1984a) *A Haunt of Fears*. London: Pluto.
—— (ed.) (1984b) *The Video Nasties: Freedom and Censorship in the Media*. London: Pluto.
Barthes, Roland (1973) *Mythologies*. Trans. Annette Lavers. St Albans: Paladin. (Originally published 1957.)
BBC (1988) *Violence and the Media*. London: BBC.
Coward, Rosalind (1984) *Female Desire: Women's Sexuality Today*. London: Paladin.
—— (1987) 'Violent Screen Play'. *Marxism Today*, December 1987: 24–7.
Creed, Barbara (1987) 'From here to modernity – feminism and postmodernism'. *Screen*, 28 (2): 46–67.

MacCabe, Colin (1988) 'The South Bank Show Lecture'. *Marxism Today*, April 1988: 27–31.

Modleski, Tania (1984) *Loving with a Vengeance: Mass Produced Fantasies for Women*. London: Methuen.

Morrell, David (1973) *First Blood*. London: Pan.

Nairn, Tom (1988) *The Enchanted Glass: Britain and its Monarchy*. London: Radius.

Webster, Duncan (1988) *Looka Yonder! The Imaginary America of Populist Culture*. London: Comedia and Routledge.

'HIGH CULTURE' REVISITED

Let's do away with critical distance!

(John Fiske)[1]

I

The late 1960s and the 1970s brought about both a substantial increase in and new forms of scholarly interest in popular culture. New approaches were marked by an interdisciplinary and 'totalizing' conception of socio-cultural research, transcending traditional boundaries between economics, politics, and aesthetics. Research was supposed to contribute to a *general* critique of (capitalist) society-as-a-whole, in theoretical and methodological matters openly guided by what Habermas (1968) once called an 'emancipatory knowledge-interest'.

This approach was clearly linked to the contemporary revival of Marxist theory, and as political conjunctures changed, the various forms of Marxist-inspired research ran into severe problems. The theoretical developments between, say, 1975 and 1985 have proved fruitful in many ways. It seems to me, though, as if the hallmark of the tradition from the 1960s – research as a contribution to 'total' social critique – is about to get lost in certain current trends in media and cultural studies, in spite of a retained 'emancipatory knowledge-interest'.

A critique of these trends sooner or later runs into the highly complex debates over 'post-modernity'/'post-modernism'. In this article, though, I will try to avoid a general discussion of the theoretical and political status of these concepts. Instead, a widely shared basic assumption within current critical media research will be looked into, and a critique of it attempted. I should at once stress that this is a highly problematic venture, and that my views are presented tentatively, open to further debate.

I should add that this article is an attempt at 'checking' the viability of certain ideas and perspectives developed during the 1960s and 1970s, consciously opposing the form of collective amnesia that a certain theoretical 'trendiness' in the fields of media and cultural studies seems to produce. The personal need to write something like this arose after spending six months in the United States, getting increasingly annoyed with the axiomatic status of certain fashionable but not entirely reliable observations on 'postmodern culture' within some academic circles. Regarding myself as in many ways some sort of 'postmodernist' in Norway, I was a bit surprised to realize that in view of certain Anglo-American discourses on media, culture, and politics, I would have to agree with Habermas that Modernity/Enlightenment is still an incomplete project.

The assumption I intend to criticize is that the distinction between high and low culture is 'in fact' outmoded and only kept alive in reactionary ideological rhetoric. In my view, the distinction is not only still alive as a social fact throughout the western world, even if the relationship(s) between the two spheres may differ considerably from one country to another and on the whole have undergone very important changes. It also seems pertinent that we have a closer look at the institutions and practices embraced by high culture, and discuss their relevance to critical research and analysis in our field(s). I then intend to argue that a total dismissal of the distinction between high and low culture may serve as an ideological veiling of the social positions of researchers and other academic intellectuals, hindering a recognition of the political limitations, obligations, and possibilities inherent in these positions.

I would like to start, though, by sketching how the tendency I am criticizing is directly linked to basic features of the 1960s' tradition. Thus I intend not only to signal my own degree of sympathy with my object of critique. The historical approach also allows for some important observations on the characteristics of the present generation of media researchers and students.

II

The early efforts of 'neo-Marxist' media research, especially within the humanities, may be labeled 'critique of ideology'. Its two main objectives represented a radical challenge to traditional notions of art and cultural heritage within academia. First, a (re)interpretation of cultural texts from both high and low culture was intended to show how the texts contained and conveyed ideology, forms of consciousness that supported social repression. Second, inextricably linked to the first, a rewriting of cultural history was undertaken which would expose class- and gender-based repression not only in society and culture in general, but in traditional academic research and writing as well. 'Digging up' artists, texts, and whole traditions of cultural expression that had been left out of traditional accounts of cultural history was a highly rewarding activity in this respect. It was easily demonstrated that the construction of cultural canons relied not only on something regarded as pure and socially neutral aesthetic and historical judgement, but also very much on certain clearly ideological notions.

Although much work on popular culture was devoted to exposing the bourgeois, misogynist etc. ideology of texts, this form of popular-culture criticism differed from earlier critical disavowal in at least two significant ways. First, popular-culture texts were analyzed with the same semiological/semiotic tools as the texts of the high culture canons – and for the same purpose: exposing ideology. Thus the methodology, based on a semiotic understanding of the nature of language and texts, in itself posed a critique of traditional aesthetic hierarchies. Second, and this may be even more crucial to an understanding of later developments, it soon became clear that the new scholarly critique of popular culture was to a considerable extent a 'critique from within'. The critical students and scholars were themselves consumers of the artifacts in question. Having grown up with pop music, movies, television etc., their position could hardly be one of totally detached, condescending distance. Their own pleasures in the consumption of popular or mass culture products had to complicate the ideological analyses sooner or later, not least because their political commitment in many cases was directly linked to their engagement with the mass mediated 'youth culture' of the 1960s, rock music in particular.[2] The uneasiness produced by these complications have in many cases led to a development Tania Modleski has formulated as follows:

> If the problem of some of the work of the Frankfurt School was that its members were too far outside the culture they examined, critics today seem to have the opposite problem: immersed in their culture, half in love with their subject, they sometimes seem unable to achieve the proper critical distance from it. As a result, they may unwittingly wind up writing apologias for mass culture and embracing its ideology. (Modleski, 1986: xi)

According to this line of thinking, the postwar baby-boomers had specific interests in a more appreciative view of mass-mediated low or popular culture. But this was not only in keeping with their own cultural experience of growing up in a society where the 'culture industry' and modern mass media dominated everyday life. To many students and younger scholars a positive re-evaluation of 'mass culture' and its recipients could also serve as a solution to a certain, specific dilemma concerning their social identity.

This function is suggested by the fact that the radicalization of students that occurred in the 1960s coincided with an unprecedented growth in the number of students at institutions of higher learning. In Norway, for instance, the number of students at the universities tripled during this decade. Even if the recruitment was socially skewed in favour of sons and daughters of academic and upper-class parents, this rapid process also meant an unprecedented influx of students from working-class or non-academic petit-bourgeois backgrounds, also often from geographically 'peripheral' areas. These people entered the realm of high culture, in which the universities are central institutions, with a newcomer's ambivalence. While university education might have been a conscious goal for most of them – and student life consequently in many ways a fulfilling experience – the prevailing complacency of the academic proponents of high culture would seem to many of them either offensive or stupid or both.

This type of cultural clash is of course not limited to the experience of students of this particular generation. It has probably been the experience of every working- or peasant-class bookworm with similar careers since the dawning of modernity. Such upwardly-mobile subjects are placed in a sort of cultural limbo, not properly integrated in the lower-class culture they left, nor in the upper-class high culture they have formally entered. Since they are newcomers, they are faced with a need to make *choices* concerning what to do in and with their acquired position. This is not given by family tradition or upper-class consciousness. One solution here could be (1) to strive for or pretend full integration into upper-class high culture, simply taking the class position opened to them by their education. Another way out of the dilemma could be (2) to strive for or pretend re-integration into the classes they once left, preferably as 'leaders' in some sense, 'voices' for the people, etc. Various radical organizations could function for them as a 'home away from home'.[3] The third, most difficult, alternative would be (3) for them to *acknowledge their marginal position* and identify themselves as intellectuals in the sense once formulated by Jean Paul Sartre: 'un-assimilated everywhere' (Sartre, 1973), and start investigating the possibilities for *engagement* from there.

It seems to me that the strategy of 'siding with' the consumers of popular culture, by more or less uncritically legitimating their choices and their presumed tastes, is often motivated by the second alternative. It is not only an act of solidarity, but also functions more self-satisfactorily as a form of symbolic 'homecoming'. The strategy offers an imaginary way out of the newborn, radical intellectual's socio-cultural limbo, often regarded with suspicion by 'the people', who at least since Romanticism have learnt to distrust intellectuals pretending to be more 'popular' than the people themselves, pretending that all those books and schools haven't changed them in any significant way.

The hermeneutic nature of any attempt at analyzing and understanding culture and society necessitates acknowledgement of and critical reflection on the socio-cultural specificity of the researcher and his/her position. My impression is that much current work in Anglo-American media and cultural studies fails to do so, by implicitly denying both the privileged and the marginal aspects of the position of the researchers. The almost ritual denunciations of high culture in much writing (and talking) within this (these) field(s) can be seen as one expression of this dilemma.

III

The rhetorical dismissals of the notion of high culture that I have in mind fail to take into consideration that the concept has several meanings. It refers both to a set of institutions, to certain types of media and texts, and to discourses on these and other social phenomena. This complex material and cultural sphere is of course constantly undergoing changes, and some of the changes over the last decades have been fundamental.[4] But if we for the moment concentrate on the institutions and discourses of high culture, a few quite stable characteristics relevant to our discussion here do emerge.

Universities and other institutions of higher learning are still, as stated above, parts of the high-culture institutional realm. This is also true of the various discourses that circulate within academic and intellectual communities, constantly referring to and presupposing a couple of thousand years of 'high' cultural history within 'Western Civilization'. In this perspective, attacks on the notion of high culture in writings about, for instance, the complex subject positions in postmodern intertextuality, appear ludicrous in their ideological blindness. They represent an implicit denial of the social determination of discourses, not least their own very obvious belonging to a high-culture discourse on culture.

Such denial may also make it hard to grasp the implications of the differences between the discourses on soap operas in *Soap Opera Digest* and those in *Screen*. Denunciation of high culture, often accompanied by populist attacks on 'elitism' (as if unequal distribution of knowledge and other resources were just another reactionary ideological fantasy), may have the dubious function of presenting the writer or speaker in question as no-different-from-the-rest, as some sort of ordinary and authentic soap-watcher-in-general.

Presenting oneself as a soap-fan in scholarly circles could be considered daring or provocative some ten years ago. Nowadays it is more of a prerequisite for legitimate entry into the academic discourse on soaps in some Anglo-American fora. The demographic profiles of soap audiences consistently suggested by surveys are not seen as demanding social explanation, but often dismissed either as produced by slightly immoral administrative information-gathering for the industry, or as 'elitist' and 'empiricist' misrepresentations of 'reality' – for instance by pointing to the popularity of soaps among certain groups of college students and other marginal audiences.[5]

The writer/researcher/critic is then left with a classless, at the most gendered, subject with equally classless pleasures in the encounter with the soap text in question. By pretending that the academic critic's pleasure is the same as anybody else's, s/he not only erases the socio-cultural differences between the academic and the genre's core audiences, but also avoids analyzing the specificities of for instance the film scholar's pleasure in soap-watching. And soap-talking!

Such specific analysis would require considerations on the differences between, on the one hand, soap-watchers with years and years devoted to the accumulation of high cultural capital in Pierre Bourdieu's sense – and on the other hand soap fans less well-off in this respect. Such considerations might render the distinction between high and low culture harder to dismiss – or overlook – in cultural analysis.

IV

So far I have only tried to demonstrate the validity of the distinction between high and low culture by linking scholarly discourses on culture to the high-culture institutions which are their material basis. Examining the distinction more thoroughly requires a closer look at the obvious changes in the relationships between the two spheres that I briefly mentioned above.

Today's university students and teachers may be devoted rock fans – while at the same time being readers of James Joyce and Friedrich Nietzsche. This kind of floating between media and genres on both sides of the high/low border is often regarded as one of the hallmarks of the 'postmodern' cultural condition. In my view, it is a historically new situation. But *structurally* it is reminiscent of Peter Burke's (1978) outline of the relationship between 'high' (upper-class/learned) culture and 'low' (lower-class, folk/traditional) culture in the middle ages. The bearers of high/learned culture would also share and participate in the competences and practices of low/popular culture, until the onset of modern thought, scientific and geographical discoveries etc. rendered the split in terms of ways of thinking/'world views'/forms of consciousness too wide. Popular (*folk*) culture was then left to itself, until it was rediscovered as something exotically 'authentic' by the Romantic movement towards the end of the eighteenth century. The concrete, historical developments of the relationships between high and low culture will vary considerably from place to place,[6] and popular/low culture is split into folk (traditional, typically rural) and 'mass' ('industrial', typically urban) culture by the advent of industrial capitalism, further complicating the use of ahistorical parallelisms. Still, the structural similarity between the situation described by Burke in relation to Europe's middle ages and today's so-called 'convergence' between high and low culture remains helpful in conceptualizing what is going on.

What the presence of the PhD at the rock concert tells us is that the audiences of the two cultural spheres overlap. But what is often overlooked, is *how* they overlap. While the audiences in the opera almost certainly go to the movies and even watch television, the majority of movie and television audiences will never go to the opera; or visit places like museums of contemporary art, certain theatres, seminars on feminism and psychoanalysis, poetry readings, or lectures by Derrida. The point I am trying to make is as simple as it is significant. Some people have access to both high and low culture, but the majority has only access to the low one. (A diminishing minority has only access to high culture – that should not be forgotten either!)

It can safely be assumed that the dividing lines between 'double-access' and 'single-access' audiences coincide with lines drawn on the basis of other significant social characteristics, such as income and education. (Age is also relevant here, as the most typical double-access audiences are probably younger than, say, 50.) In other words, the reception of high and low culture is still clearly linked to the social formations we call classes. The double access to the codes and practices of both high and low culture is a *class privilege*. Consequently, denial of the existence of significant differences between high and low culture is ideological in the most simplistic Marxist sense – it engenders ideas serving to conceal inequality in the distribution of power and other resources. Just like the traditional bourgeois wanted (wants!) us to believe that 'money means nothing, we're all equal', certain theorists of culture now want us to believe that 'knowing Aristotle, Shakespeare, Marx, Foucault and Godard means nothing, we're all equal'.

Admittedly, money (economic capital) is very different from cultural knowledge/capital. While money is universally recognized as a key to a better life, most people don't give a damn about Godard; or about Aristotle, Marx, or Foucault for that matter. And they are of course right, in the sense that you don't necessarily get a more secure, comfortable, or even enjoyable life out of having access to high culture, its codes and products. It may even be more probable that the more you know of it, the gloomier you get (one may think of Hegel's 'unhappy consciousness' and related forms of intellectual melancholia . . .). So why bother?

V

This is where the harder part of my argument starts. I am supposed to argue that something not necessarily enjoyable is worth having. In other words, I am now moving into the *qualitative* aspect of the 'high-culture' concept. What I have done so far has only been to point to the existence of an inescapable hierarchy of classes and a roughly parallel hierarchy of cultural formations and forms which cannot be transcended by individual word-acts alone. The question of whether qualitative differences between cultural forms can be hierarchically ordered as well is far more complicated. It is a lot easier and also more rewarding (to me at least) to tear down socially constructed hierarchies (which I have tried to contribute to for years) than to defend them.

It would be impossible here to discuss the multiple attempts at establishing 'objective' criteria for the evaluation of aesthetic artifacts. But I do want to point out that the question of aesthetic quality has been neglected for too long within the various fields of critical media studies – not to mention traditional mass communication research.[7] As traditional canons and hierarchies of values have been rightfully deconstructed, a combination of programmatic relativism and tacit agreement on taste has made anything but very widely conceived *political* criteria of evaluation unspeakable. And even the political criteria are losing ground, in two ways. First, the 'discovery' that texts are not univocal but offer possibilities for 'oppositional', 'aberrant', or even 'subversive' readings has undermined any simplistic notion of texts as mere vehicles of ideology. Second, the current enthusiasm for ethnographic reception studies can produce some very odd conclusions. Thus a critical analysis of *Rambo* concluding that it is a reactionary movie might be argued, by ethnographers, to be somehow 'displaced' by their finding that a particular audience sub-group has produced a reading of the film as an enjoyable anti-establishment (?) epic.[8]

Even if most traditional notions of Art may seem more or less impossible to uphold, I would at least argue that the relationship between *knowledge* and *judgement* may be worth some further discussion.

Such a discussion could start with a commonsensical assumption: it is not improbable that a literary scholar's judgement about a piece of literature is in some sense more qualified than that of any individual reader without the critic's training and experience. This is only more or less equivalent to saying that a carpenter (or a designer, or someone professionally teaching carpenters and designers) is in some sense the best judge of carpentry. The possibility that individual readers' experience of the piece in question may differ completely from the scholar's does not contradict this principle, no more than my appreciation of a piece of furniture which a carpenter regards with contempt. The parallel between texts and furniture should of course not be taken too far, but the element of experience and knowledge in a critic's work should not be completely disregarded either. Pretending that years of specialized training in criticism has not taught us anything about how to distinguish a well-done piece of 'art' from a not-so-well-done one, is futile. More important, however, is that this training should also have taught us to explicate the various criteria for our judgement, thus making the evaluation accessible for discussion and contestation.

Furthermore, the academic critic's conclusions about a text are sup-posedly based on some sort of analysis of the text in question, an interpretative effort aimed at bringing to the fore dimensions of the text not necessarily consciously accessible through the normal, once-over reading. This is to argue that the outcome of a reading based on textual analysis can only be contested by other readings based on analytic work on/with the text. This elementary principle is of course terribly 'elitist', but still indispensible for any kind of socio-cultural analysis that wants to move beyond mere registration of 'facts': interpretative work necessarily privileges the inter-preter. The validity of its results can not be determined by simple 'checking of the facts' or by counting the number of individuals who agree. Rather, it depends upon the sophistication of procedures and the quality of arguments – and on whether or not one shares the (preferably) explicated, moral, and political values the interpreting subject carries with her/him when encoun-tering the text.

Aesthetic values always have moral and political components (cf. Mukarovsky, 1979). But they have other components too, criteria for the evaluation of various aspects of 'craftsmanship'. This is why anti-fascists are able to see that Leni Riefenstahl's *Triumph des Willens* is a well-done film – even though they may still find it ideologically repulsive. To draw the line(s) between 'craftsmanship' and ideology at a general, theoretical level is practically impossible, since texts in all media that are intended to voice something 'oppositional' in some sense (or just 'different from the rest') will often have to break with established uses of each medium's means of expression. But those of us who, like me, have done extensive research on 'forgotten' textual traditions (workers' literature, for example) will know that history is full of texts that are definitely lousy from almost every possible point of view, especially when they are extracted from their immediate socio-historical context. If someone sets out to write a sonnet, a strongly defined form of poetic expression, there should be a discernible/constructable artistic *idea* explaining or giving sense to breaks with the sonnet's form. If not, it's sheer sloppiness, a failure – no matter which philosophical, moral, or political values it may attempt to convey. Critical training should, in principle, increase the reader's ability to discern failure from creativity, a judgement that always requires a consideration of plausible intentions and of context. Valid judgements of this kind presup-pose quite extensive knowledge of the medium in question and of the various relevant contextual elements. Feminist films may not (should not?) adhere to

Hollywood standards, but a 'lousy shot' may be either just a lousy shot or an element in some kind of textual strategy relevant to the aesthetico-political project in question.

The point I am (tentatively) trying to make here, is that aesthetic judgements made by members of a more or less academic community of critics and/or practitioners may well be regarded as the most solidly founded, in the sense that they are based on specialized training and knowledge. The teaching of literature, theatre, film etc. in schools at all levels also necessarily requires choices from the enormous mass of texts available, and if sales or audience figures are not to be the only criteria for the choices made, some standards for judging 'quality' or 'degree of interest' must be established, preferably based on a kind of knowledge not yet possessed by students.[9]

This does on the other hand *not* mean that these specialists should have some sort of social authority that gives them the unrestricted right to prescribe a certain cultural menu to people outside their own group or class outside the classroom, for instance through the public broadcasting channels that rule the airwaves in countries like the Scandinavian. But such a view of differences in aesthetic qualifications allows us to keep the distinction between more or less 'naive' and more or less 'informed' receptions of texts, even if a unilinear hierarchy of the texts themselves is considered an impossible idea.[10] It also implies that the kind of competence the critic possesses may be desirable for others, in so far as they want to know more about a particular area. The general musical competence of a musicologist may be of interest to young rock musicians who want to know more about what they are in fact doing and what they might be able to achieve by way of a 'technical' language. (The musicologist may be even more useful to rock musicians if he is aware of the limits of traditional musicology in dealing with the rock idiom.)

There is then, in my view, some general value in the kinds of knowledge that *also* distinguish people with 'cultural capital', that is, people with access to high culture's texts and discourses. There is power in this kind of knowledge as much as there is in others. Furthermore, the academic/ intellectual discourses on culture and the arts are strongly linked to the more general discourses on society, politics, economics, health etc. – in a multitude of ways. The language(s) of high culture belong to the dominant discourses in society, specialized in refined abstract thought and (potentially) instrumental reason. Mastering them is part of general social mastery, of gaining and executing social power. This is *one* reason why high culture remains a sphere worth conquering for those in less powerful positions than ours, and why the traditional 'distributive' idea in the cultural politics favoured by the social democratic labour movement retains some political relevance.

Another reason might simply be that as lower classes still are, in practice, excluded from much of the high-culture realm, the historical point once made about working-class appropriation of high culture still holds some truth. As long as the working class is excluded from high culture, then 'even the canonization of classical art and literature [by workers' organizations, JG] contained democratizing, antiauthoritarian, yes: heretic impulses' (Brückner and Ricke, 1974: 41).[11]

Such 'impulses' gain subversive significance at another level, when the process of appropriation of high culture by previously excluded groups produces insights both into cultural history in general and the concrete experiences and conditions of the subjects in question.[12] The appropriation of high culture might also be an appropriation of history, of an 'expanded' historical consciousness – provided that the process is of a critical, self-reflective kind. Such a perspective would raise a number of questions – what are the limitations of 'high culture'? how does it relate to our own social and existential experiences? how does the sensual and emotional 'impact' of the poem, performance, picture in question relate to the 'impact' of artifacts from other cultural traditions? Such questions can only be asked from an 'outsider's' position – an outsider in the process of establishing knowledge of the 'inside' and 'the insiders': questions asked by *critical intellectuals*.

VI

Pierre Bourdieu's work on the sociology of culture contains provocative and enlightening analyses of the 'economic' logic of the intellectual field. The analysis suggests that all struggles within this field are 'actually' just struggles for positions of power within the field, that nothing but the participants' positions and interests are at stake in cultural debates, research, etc. The energy and significance(s) of Bourdieu's own sustained efforts suggest something else, though, something his purely 'structural' approach cannot really thematize. His demystifying, critical research must not only be driven by some kind of 'emancipatory knowledge-interest', but also be based on substantial knowledge of various forms of both high and low culture: his own extraordinary amount of cultural capital. In my view, this clearly implies that 'cultural capital' is not 'empty', devoid of substance and quality, like the completely abstract exchange value of economic capital. Cultural capital is not reducible to its abstract function as vehicle for individual intellectual careers: it always has a use-value in which there are ties to more general social interests.

Another aspect of the use-value of cultural capital may be what Bourdieu calls 'pure' taste. While the 'barbaric' taste, which Bourdieu argues is characteristic of the lower classes, insists on 'the continuity between art and life, which implies the subordination of form to function', 'pure' taste has as its basic premise the separation of the aesthetic from other aspects of life, so that the aesthetic demands a particular form of distanciation, in order to be apprehended adequately (Bourdieu, 1984: 32). While 'barbaric' taste – and products directed at satisfying it – prefers direct emotional involvement, sensual pleasure, and priority to 'content' over 'form', 'pure' taste – and its corresponding products – demands detachment, distanciation, reflection, and tends to focus on 'form' rather than 'content', D. W. Griffith's formulation of the difference between 'European' and 'American' films refers to the same difference in tastes – while the typically American film says 'come and *have* an experience', the typically 'European' film says 'come and *see* an experience' (Monaco, 1981: 36).

If pure taste may thus be said to demand a distanciating attitude, it seems to me that this parallels the intellectual distanciation which is a prerequisite for all forms of critical reflection (and thus for conscious, 'strategic' political action as well). Pure taste's distanciating critical discourse has, in the postwar period, been able to appropriate originally 'barbaric' cultural forms in film, music, and various print media. This indicates not only that the categorization of particular forms of texts on either side of the high/low border has something historically 'accidental' about it, that there is a fluidity between the high and low realms of culture in the area of 'artistic' texts. It also indicates the real freedom and power of the high-culture discourse. The everyday language used in everyday talk about soap operas, movies, and pop music is not useful as a means to a refined understanding of most high culture texts. But, as Bourdieu's work shows, the high culture discourse can even distanciate itself from itself.[13] This ability is its critical potential.

VII

To sum up my argument: high and low culture are still separated cultural realms in terms of institutions, discourses, and, to a large extent, also in terms of traditions of cultural ('artistic') expression. Students and researchers of culture clearly have their base in the high-culture realm, and should reflect on this as a basic premise for critical work in their various fields. Our ability to take part in both high and low culture's codes and practices is a class privilege; it does not mean that the socially operative distinction between the two spheres have ceased to exist. High culture remains a sphere worth conquering for those now excluded from it, not least because of the critical potential of its meta-languages. It is our task as critical intellectuals to draw on this potential in order to turn our inescapable social distance from other categories of people into a critical one, serving an 'emancipatory knowledge-interest'.

While doing so, we may as recipients of any available cultural product benefit from the pleasures of the hard-to-pin-down phenomenon 'art' (a three-letter-word in some recent forms of critical media studies), in accordance with Brecht's cunning statement:

> Even when there is talk of higher and lower forms of amusement, art keeps a straight face, because it wishes to move both high and low and be left alone, as long as it can entertain people by doing so. (Brecht, 1973: 111)

University of Bergen, Norway

Notes

1 Enthusiastic remark by John Fiske in a discussion following a presentation by Ien Ang at the International Communications Association's conference in Montreal, May 1987.

2 I owe this last point, that rock and folk music, for large sections of the radical 1960s generation, was an integral part of becoming and being politically conscious, to Michael Schudson, who kindly gave valuable comments on an earlier draft of this article.

3 Stuart Hall wrote in a review of Raymond Williams' *Politics And Letters* (1979):

> I still feel a strong sympathy for that way in which the bright young lad from the 'periphery', coming to Oxbridge as the idealized pinnacle of an *intellectual* path, first experiences the actual *social* shock of discovering that Oxbridge is not only the apex of official English intellectual culture, but the cultural centre of the class system. I know at once what Williams means by remarking, in his usual understated way, that 'the class stamp of Trinity was not difficult to spot'; and also that inevitable path which led, in the search for some kind of refuge, to the discovery of the Socialist Club – 'a home away from home'. (Hall, 1980: 96)

The utopian dream of successful reintegration as 'homecoming', carried by radical intellectuals with lower-class backgrounds, is the central figure of thought identified and discussed in my book on a nationalist-democratic mass movement in Norway, *Folkeopplysningas dialektikk* ('The dialectics of popular enlightenment'), in press. The basic structure of this dream is that The People have borne a Son, who Leaves Home in order to acquire Knowledge, which The Son then brings back to The People, creating the dialectical *Aufhebung* which enables the People to realize their True Essence or Historical Role (*Wesen*). My book deals not least with the various problems that arises when this Dream is confronted with Reality, i.e. the *resistance* from The People against their self-appointed representatives.

4 I am here thinking of phenomena such as high-culture 'appropriation' of low-culture artifacts and textual traditions since the 1950s (jazz and Hollywood films, in France) and 1960s (for instance pop art, in the US and elsewhere); and the changes in the social composition of audiences within the two spheres which I discuss below.

5 Robert C. Allen's highly valuable book, *Speaking of Soap Operas* (1985), gives a very critical account of the quantitative research on soap-opera audiences. This research has, since the 1930s, demonstrated that soaps are relatively *more* popular with lower-class and female audiences than with upper-class and male audiences. Allen's point is that research *also* shows that soaps are enjoyed by people of all social classes and both genders, a fact investigators often have left out of consideration in order to 'collapse the entire soap opera audience into a single social and psychosocial category whose members could be regarded as "different" from everyone else' (p. 28). His argument for the complexity of the audience (and the soap opera itself) is acceptable, and especially understandable when regarded as polemic against the simplistic tradition of US empiricism in mass communication research. The problem is that Allen does not seem to regard the consistency of the audience pattern marking certain social categories as *more* interested in soaps than others as a phenomenon in need of a

socio-cultural explanation. In less sophisticated versions than Allen's, the critique of empiricism may be turned into a dismissal of all reasoning on the significance of observed affinities between specific social categories/classes and specific genres like the soap opera.

6 Paul DiMaggio's (1986) admirably lucid and thorough account of the establishment of high-culture institutions in Boston in the second half of the nineteenth century demonstrates this. His analysis shows how a certain bourgeois group (the Brahmins) established distinct high-culture institutions, which brought an end to previous fora for mixed cultural presentations to equally mixed audiences. Still, pertinent to my argument: (a) DiMaggio's analysis does *not* show that the older mixed presentations of, for instance, 'high' and 'low' forms of music were not *experienced* as mixed, i.e. that the audiences at these 'pre-split' gatherings were not already split in terms of tastes; (b) the Brahmins' preference for "high" culture forms may (should) be understood as part of a class strategy for establishing socio-cultural distinction, but the choice of high culture for this purpose is not accidental. It is related not only to the abstract social status of this culture (in this case imported from Europe), but *also* to *qualitative* characteristics of the various high-culture forms: their relatedness and affinity to the tradition of modern learned culture and advanced thought in general.

7 As Adorno (1973) pointed out in his *Résümé über Kulturindustrie*: 'Because of its [the culture industry's, JG] role in society, uneasy questions concerning its quality, concerning truth or untruth, concerning its aesthetic status are suppressed or at least kept out of the so-called sociology of communication.'

8 For a very different interpretation of this phenomenon see Fiske (1987: 316).

9 Cf. Schudson 1987, especially pp. 66f.

10 Something in the way of a 'multilinear hierarchy of genres' may be a tenable idea, though, i.e. an ordering of genres according to what they can and cannot 'do' or 'hold' in terms of themes and modes of dealing with themes. There are limits to what a soap opera can contribute to a serious discussion of Death And Its Implications.

11 I should stress here that Brückner and Ricke refer to the times (end of the nineteenth century) when the working class was *openly* excluded from various bourgeois cultural events, fora, and forms. It seems to me, though, that their argument may be valid for our times too, when exclusion is informal but still very real.

12 Such an exemplary educational 'use' of high culture is described by the German-Swedish writer Peter Weiss in his three-volume novel *Ästhetik des Widerstands* (The Aesthetics of Resistance) (1975–8, published also in the three Scandinavian languages). Jürgen Habermas' rendering of the example should demonstrate my point:

Weiss describes the process of reappropriating art by presenting a group of politically motivated, knowledge-hungry workers in 1937 in Berlin. These were young people who, through an evening high school education, acquired the intellectual means to fathom the general and social history of European art. Out of the resilient edifice of this objective mind, embodied in works of art which they saw again and again in the museums of Berlin, they started removing their own chips of stone, which they gathered together and reassembled in the context of their own milieu. This milieu was far removed from that of traditional education as well as from the then existing regime. These young workers went back and forth between the edifice of European art and their own milieu until they were able to illuminate both. (Habermas, 1985: 13)

13 Cf. Bourdieu's closing remark in his preface to the English language edition of *Distinction*:

At all events, there is nothing more universal than the project of objectifying the mental structures associated with the particularity of a social structure. Because it presupposes an epistemological break which is also a social break, a sort of estrangement from the familiar, domestic, native world, the critique (in the Kantian sense) of culture invites each reader, through the 'making strange' beloved of the Russian Formalists, to reproduce, on his or her own behalf, the critical break of which it is the product. For this reason it is perhaps the only rational basis for a truly universal culture. (Bourdieu, 1984: xiv)

References

Adorno, T. W. (1973) 'Om kulturindustrien' (On the culture industry), in H. F. Dahl (ed.) *Massekommunikasjon*. Oslo: Gyldendal. (Originally published 1967.)

Allen, R. C. (1985) *Speaking of Soap Operas*, Chapel Hill: University of North Carolina Press.

Bourdieu, P. (1984) *Distinction*. Cambridge, Mass.: Harvard University Press. (Originally published 1979.)

Brecht, B. (1973) *Lille Organon for teatret* (Little Organon for the Theater), in B. Brecht, *Om tidens teater*. Copenhagen: Gyldendal. (Originally published 1948.)

Brückner, P. and Ricke, G. (1974) 'Über die ästhetische Erziehung des Menschen in der Arbeiterbewegung', in C. Bezzel *et al. Das Unvermögen der Realität. Beiträge zu einer anderen materialistischen Ästhetik*. Berlin: Verlag Klaus Wagenbach.

Burke, P. (1978) *Popular Culture in Early Modern Europe*. Hounslow: Temple Smith.

DiMaggio, P. (1986) 'Cultural entrepreneurship in nineteenth century Boston: the creation of an organizational base for high culture in America', in R. Collins *et al.* (eds) *Media, Culture and Society*. Beverly Hills, Newbury Park, New Delhi: Sage.

Fiske, J. (1987) *Television Culture*. London: Methuen.

Habermas, J. (1968) *Technik und Wissenschaft als 'Ideologie'*. Frankfurt: Suhrkamp Verlag.

Habermas, J. (1985) 'Modernity – an incomplete project', in H. Foster (ed.) *Postmodern Culture*. London: Pluto.

Hall, S. (1980) 'The Williams Interviews'. *Screen Education*, 34 (Spring): 94–104.

Modleski, T. (1986) Introduction in her (ed.) *Studies in Entertainment*. Bloomington: Indiana University Press.

Monaco, J. (1981) *How to Read a Film*. New York and Oxford: Oxford University Press.

Mukarovsky, J. (1979) 'Estetisk verdi som sosialt faktum' (Aesthetic value as a social fact), in A. Heldal and A. Linneberg (eds) *Strukturalisme i litteraturvitenskapen*. Oslo: Gyldendal. (Originally published 1936.)

Sartre, J. P. (1973) 'Forsvar for de intellektuelle', in *Vinduet*, 23 (2): 3–23. (Norw. translation of two lectures, published in *Plaidoyer pour les intellectuals*, Paris 1972: Gallimard.)

Schudson, M. (1987) 'The new validation of popular culture: sense and sentimentality in academia', in *Critical Studies in Mass Communication*, 4: 51–68.

GIRL MEETS BOY: AESTHETIC PRODUCTION, RECEPTION, AND GENDER IDENTITY

Mention video, and people start talking about the young. This is not surprising. Video is perhaps the most directly influential of the new media, and its influence is felt chiefly by children and adolescents who are among its keenest users.[1] And unlike older viewers, the cultural identities of the young are being shaped in a thoroughly visual era.

Since the early 1980s, when video first found a mass market in western Europe, public debates on video have focused on 'the nasties', on video violence and its alleged ill-effects on the innocent minds of the under-age. With almost tedious accuracy, the moral panic in most countries spirals into demands for firm policies banning the worst excrescences in the volatile video business.[2] Concerned social workers, committed teachers, and critics have entered the debate with the express aim to counteract received notions of children and young people as a generation of would-be criminals imitating their hardhitting screen heroes or visual zombies devouring pictures more desperately than the gruesome characters' devouring of victims: crime, the critics stress, is rooted in social and psychological structures more profound and complex than the watching of videos, and most youngsters are not the television addicts envisaged by the media hysteria.

Professional research on youth and video has emphasized two main aspects: (1) investigations of video consumption – what do adolescents see and why? (Roe and Salmonsen, 1983; Glogauer, 1988); (2) studies on media education – how can we make the young better, that is more critical, viewers? (Halloran and Jones, 1985; Masterman, 1985). Tackling those questions *are* pertinent, not least in Scandinavia where our long tradition of public-service media is currently being challenged by satellite and cable channels.[3] For good reasons, then, public debates and professional discussion have stressed the commercial videos and their reception.

But at the same time, many young people use video in different ways that have almost entirely escaped serious adult attention. The video boom has more or less coincided with an unprecedented growth of cultural production, shaped by a variety of adolescents outside the confines of flamboyant subcultures and avant-garde counter-cultures. Undoubtedly influenced by these visible groups, a growing number of 'ordinary' adolescents today experiment with media such as community radio, video and home computing, with musicals, modern dance, and rock music to a degree that not even the garage bands of the Beatles, or indeed the punk waves could envisage. Youth clubs, public media centres, and local activity houses may form institutional backdrops to these activities.[4] But often they are part of informal and changing peer-group relations. Seen from a Scandinavian perspective, this growing interest is characterized by certain trends: (1) popular cultural forms are of focal concern (video, rock music, comics); (2) middle-class adolescents form key members in the self-styled groups; (3) girls occupy a central position within many of these cultural spaces.

To my knowledge, no surveys have documented the range of these cultural activities on a larger scale. But the above trends are borne out by my own work with adolescents and their video production. The impetus to this work was the glaring contradiction between adult and adolescent interests: while we concentrate upon their reception of the commercial media, many of the young are busy trying out those media for themselves. How do boys and girls use video? What are their productions like? What do those activities mean to them? Answering these questions may help us elucidate a blind spot in current media research. But the answers also throw into relief larger issues: what are the conditions of cultural production made by ordinary people in an age of post-industrial development? What are the implications of this production for cultural and media studies? While my own work does not resolve these complex questions, it is hoped that the following analysis may open a forum for further discussion.

The video project

For about a year I have followed a group aged 14–17 who made a video in a Danish youth school (*ungdomsskole*).[5] These schools are a mixture of a youth club and an evening class. Open to 14–18-year-olds, these free schools are spread throughout the country and frequented by a national average of about 70 per cent of the age group. In smaller communities, the youth schools together with sports and perhaps scouting form the only organised leisure options for the young. They are open in the evenings, many arrange social events such as weekend discos, and most have pool rooms and bars where people hang around, buying soft drinks, meeting friends, and chatting up possible partners.

Originally intended as an optional training for the 'intelligence reserve' of statutory school-leavers, Danish youth schools now operate as age-bound social centres for adolescents, most of whom – like my video group – are still at school, living at home, and earning often good money for personal spending with a variety of part-time jobs. The public funding of the schools is dependent upon their annual intake of 'pupils' and so their teachers develop a keen consumer consciousness that is now further enhanced by the decrease in the number of adolescents. Thus, in 'my' school, a large one located in a socially mixed but 'nice' suburb of Copenhagen, one might find courses in about eighty different topics ranging from computer programming and French to deep-sea diving, skateboard training, personal grooming – and video. Non-academic courses were by far the most popular in this as in other youth schools.

The video course that I followed had eight or ten regular participants, three of them girls, and all of them white except one boy from Turkey. (Cultural differences and language problems made him peripheral to the group activities.) Why did they choose this course? Some had tried to use video a bit at school or at home, one had media experience from community radio that he wanted to 'put into pictures', as he said, and three belonged to the 25 per cent of Danish homes owning a VCR. Pia, who had an interest in technical matters, gave as her reason for coming that she was irritated that she 'did not really know what all those different buttons were for' on her parents' video camera. The group's immediate interest was to play around with the equipment and experiment with its different uses. This was also the aspect emphasized by their young, male teacher. Professional films were included as objects of analysis and technical guidance: how is suspense created? which angles are shown in a woman falling, etc? The course ended with a group production of a 20-minute video story. This also marked an end to my involvement with the group. I had quickly been accepted as the odd but rather uninteresting person in the corner – from what I could make out and from their teacher's information, the group was too involved in its own activities to take much notice of me. Apart from my extended observations, I interviewed the participants individually either at home or, if they did not want that, at the school.

The process

Both boys and girls initially saw video as a technical and hence a male medium. Not unexpectedly, I found that without adult direction the boys would take charge of the lighting, the props, and the camerawork. Pia, whose best school subject was maths, never meddled with technical details but was a keen actress. But so were several of the boys. As Paul put it: 'I like to be behind the camera if I cannot be in front of it.' With feminist equanimity, I took these differences as yet another proof of male dominance. But Pia put me right. For a year she was the only girl in her comprehensive school to take a course in electronics. There she had been fighting the boys who would always direct the experiments and who, she said, 'put wet sponges in my hair and chalk on my dress. . . . Our teacher only laughed. I did not find that terribly funny.' She obviously did not want to continue struggling in her leisure time too. Although she liked 'fiddling around with things' and had never learned to knit (she found it a 'passive' preoccupation), she saw the boys' technical dominance in the video course as no problem. 'Did you know there would be so many boys in the course?' I asked her, probing what I defined as a possible problem. 'No, and this was not the only reason I came', was her reply. Too many boys can evidently be a good thing when you are 15.

Gender differences were not only a hardware issue, however. They were apparent also in group discussions over small test productions as well as in the planning of the final video. The group was usually given a free rein with their ideas although the teacher would intervene if he disliked their suggestions. Everybody agreed that the long video should be fictional – real-life problems were ruled out as stupid. It should also have a story, a plot. These are youngsters who like watching the decentred narratives of pop videos, but who are less interested in experimenting with avant-garde forms in their own productions. So, something was to happen, but what? Naturally, their various answers depended upon their individual genre preferences. And not unnaturally, these corresponded to well-known gender differences in visual reception: the girls wanted realism touched up with romance, while the boys favoured action and suspense. Their mutual discussions and negotiations over a common plot were among the most exciting for themselves, and for me too. For the planning demonstrated very vividly their differences in visual pleasure.

The girls were very adamant and very inventive in advancing a girl-meets-boy theme, but they were hesitant in pushing the romance elements. The boys did not rule out the girls' suggestions. But their immediate reaction was to rephrase the girl-meets-boy theme into an *obstacles*-to-girl-meets-boy theme. They clearly distanced themselves from empathy and emotional involvement, and they did so by concentrating upon violent and comic situations. The boys went off in a virtual brainstorm of possible gags (sound effects were much enjoyed) demonstrating a mastery of genre conventions – car crashes, drownings, stranglings – from *Dirty Harry* and *Police Academy* to *Rambo* and *Alien*.[6] The girls attempted to check them by reference to reality ('this would never really happen, you know') while the teacher checked them by reference to realization ('you cannot make this happen, you know').

The common appeal of the girl-meets-boy theme highlights how self-defined video production is cultural production in the specific sense of *aesthetic production*: it makes visible pertinent problems and hidden desires by giving them concrete aesthetic form. The aesthetic process is contradictory because the feelings involved are contradictory. Developing one's sexuality is naturally seminal to adolescence. Sexual experimentation is a source of profound pleasure. But the deep emotions involved are also threatening because they may be felt to overwhelm an unstable identity (Blos, 1962). Making video opened a safe space in which the participants could act out, test, and negotiate these contradictory experiences. It was safe because it was fictional, it was not 'about' the participants, and it was negotiable because its creative energy was pleasure: the group made video to have fun, not to have their problems solved.

Crucially, the aesthetic creation was a gender-specific process of signification. The girls clearly feared violence, and the aggressive expressions of sexuality associated with violence, while the boys feared tenderness. The group found a common aesthetic meeting ground in a plot combining humour with realism and excluding violence and romance. It is inviting to speculate on the popularity of comedy in prime-time television, for example, as a result of similar gender negotiations played out over the years through the rating system. Many sit-coms, for example, combine the family focus of women's afternoon shows with the rapid pace of late-night crime movies often enjoyed by male audiences. Comedy, by mediating between typical male and female genres, is accepted by men and women alike.

The gender differences were also evident in the shooting situations. These naturally offered the real testing grounds for role playing. Here, the girls were generally most explicit about intimate emotions and some of them openly enjoyed flirting in front of the camera – and with the boy behind it. The boys used a wider range of bodily expressions, jumping about, laughing loudly, and gesturing wildly. They were also eager to teach the girls ('I'll show you. I'm an expert in falling'). At the planning stage, both boys and girls had shown a vivid imagination for details, if of different kinds.[7] Now the girls restrained themselves from putting their ideas into action. Unlike the boys, they wanted to rehearse what to say, when to move, and how to leave the scenes. This was not just a result of the girls being in the minority. For they opposed the boys in other situations. More centrally, the girls differentiated between talk and action. This may have to do with a specific pleasure in language that is nurtured in many girls' upbringing and which is central to their relations to one another in adolescence. So, while they would contradict the boys, they did not counteract them: their sexual play was clearly a body language exercised as an exciting form of communication, not as a point of intervention. The boys were generally more playful during takes and less afraid of making a fool of themselves in front of their friends: 'Oh, I'm so beautiful', Paul would remark only half-jokingly when parading his small 14-year-old figure in front of the camera and the group in obvious narcissistic enjoyment.

The boys' playfulness was demonstrated one night when Paul and his friend, in testing the white balance of the camera, started a send up of advertisements. While Paul combed his hair, all big smiles, the cameraman said in imitation of a commercial intonation: 'And here we see Model '87 with the diffuse look in his eyes. He naturally uses the deodorant . . . Williams.' (Both laugh). As in young children's role-playing, the boys elegantly switched between different levels of 'reality'. Their mutual understanding of the commercial codes left them free to improvise on and parody them. At the same time, they clearly liked the acting as such (Paul took much pleasure in his personal grooming). Moreover, they displayed their dependence upon a consumer consciousness that advertisements generally enhance. (At least in Denmark, Williams is regarded as a typical low-budget brand).

The small scene demonstrates a common pattern of action. It reveals an opposition between the boys' need for approval through commercial *integration* and their mastery of commercial clichés shown by their commercial *experimentation*: in that opposition lies the source of their laughter. But the opposition has a wider significance. It is the very standardization of commercials that allows the boys' improvisation. What many media critics and well-intentioned adults denounce as stereotypical trash, to these adolescents form a mutual reservoir of emblems fuelling their imagination and creating a collective framework of interpretation. The clichés become pieces in the construction of a variety of narrative jig-saw puzzles.

Judging from other video projects I know of, this playing with advertisements seems very common when children and young people begin making videos. The visual competences displayed, I think, challenge received theories of creativity in adolescence. These theories are chiefly derived from developmental psychology and are generally based upon a normative understanding of aesthetics as artistic expression: for example, unlike young children, most adolescents tend to draw the same objects over and over again while perfecting the details of what they draw. Taken out of the contexts in which they are put forth, such efforts seem 'mere' imitations made by passive and unimaginative individuals.[8] My boys may have been poor at drawing, but they were certainly creative in other aesthetic fields.

Perhaps the clearest indication of the group's visual competences was their unwillingness to write scripts. They adamantly resisted their teacher's attempts to have them put their ideas on paper. 'We'll just decide when we get so far.' And so they would. The result was not MTV, but it was video. Naturally, this unwillingness partly stems from an opposition to tasks bearing the slightest resemblance to school work. But the relative success of this process equally demonstrates that, symbolically speaking, the participants carried possible scripts around in their heads including an intuitive knowledge of camera angles, lighting, and music. Brought up in a world saturated with visual media, they know about them without realizing it, so to speak. Asked about scripts, Ron stated that 'writing it all down restrains you because you cannot possibly get all your wild ideas down in some script. . . . It might take you half an hour to just write down one stupid scene, see.'

Having witnessed the group's reluctance to harness the flow of their imagination, I expected them to find shooting a boring anti-climax to discussions. The pace in actually making a video is very different from planning, or indeed watching, one. But they generally concentrated during reruns of scenes as much as they would the first time. Often a sequence had to be repeated because of their laughter. Then they would start all over again as serious as before and enjoying the formalities of production ('ready, take five'). As is the case when children play, seriousness and fun were aspects of the *same* process.

As long as both these aspects were present, the group's pleasure in the process overruled the frustrations involved in having to ditch some of their marvellous ideas, of waiting around, or cancelling a scene because of rain. Significantly, the editing of the tapes – an essential element to the finished product – was performed by only two or three boys. While they were concerned with the end-product and wanted other friends to see it and to approve of it, the group clearly considered the process to be the most important and enjoyable aspect of their work.

Everyday aesthetics

This emphasis upon the process rather than the product is a key point of distinction. The video-making of 'my' group is only one example of the aesthetic production performed by people as part of their everyday cultures. If *everyday life* can be said, with the Austrian sociologist Alfred Schutz, to appear as 'the world of directly experienced social reality' (Schutz, 1972: 163; see also Lefebvre, 1971),[9] then *everyday cultures* can be defined as social symbolizations of our immediate, and often contradictory, experiences. Following this definition, we may understand *aesthetic production* as those elements of our everyday cultures in which we create symbols, and hence meaning, by giving these symbols concrete form. According to Christiaan Hart Nibbrig, such an everyday aesthetics is a 'realisation *as* materialisation [*ein Erkennen* als *Darstellen*]. This materialisation makes one realise hidden experiences that are now revealed to be unique precisely by their specific and concrete realisation.' (Nibbrig, 1978: 11). Thus, aesthetic production is not only found within drama, painting, writing, or singing. It may also be expressed through popular forms such as fashion, makeup, and rock music, or through interior decoration, painting motorbikes, even preparing a meal.

Everyday aesthetics is not limited to certain 'artistic' areas of life, it is a specific way of perceiving the world and understanding ourselves. The group of adolescents I followed made tangible their various anxieties, aspirations, and desires, not by sitting down describing and discussing them, but by making pictures and narratives fuelled by these emotions. What this process meant to them I shall return to in a moment. But to better understand the personal implications, let us dwell a bit on the concept of aesthetics.

Although rooted in antiquity, the idea of aesthetics as we know it today is shaped by modernity. During the eighteenth and nineteenth centuries, aesthetics split in two directions: one a philosophical discipline of reception, developed chiefly by Hegel and Kant, the other a norm of artistic production (in Britain, for example, Sir Joshua Reynolds and Matthew Arnold were key proponents). For our purpose, the important implications of this dichotomy are the distanciation of aesthetics from everyday experience and the concomitant specialization of aesthetics as a sphere for experts (and hence an area of education). Aesthetic reception becomes our distanced contemplation of the sublime, while aesthetics as a norm of production denotes the qualities of art created by a specially gifted minority. Aesthetics is viewed as a harmonious realm of the mind opposed to political strife and personal struggle, and transcending the concrete details of mundane reality.

In opposition to the inherent social and sexual elitism of this aesthetic tradition, the concept of an everyday aesthetics has been advanced from two professional fields on the Continent. Aesthetic theory has been reinterpreted by the so-called Budapest School of philosophy (Heller and Fehér, 1986), and in West Germany cultural critics and art-school teachers have developed the term 'everyday aesthetics' with a view to its practical, pedagogical uses (Ehmer, 1979; Hartwig, 1980; Criegern, 1982; Otto, 1984). Despite some differences, certain characteristics stand out from these recent developments: (1) everyday aesthetics is regarded as a process encompassing both production and reception and engaged in by everybody; (2) it is lodged within everyday cultures and their contradictions; (3) aesthetic production is always a concrete process; (4) it does not transcend reality, nor does it merely reflect reality, but it may refract our experiences of ordinary reality in new ways.[10] Bearing these characteristics in mind, what then did video-making imply to 'my' group of adolescents?

Aftereffects

Apart from a training in specific technical and practical skills, both boys and girls stressed that the video course had changed their modes of visual reception:

Like how the heads are placed in the picture, that sort of thing, how [the film] is made, all the presentations of characters and such . . . (Anne)

I think it's so interesting to see how a film is actually created, with camera angles and all that, and all the possibilities you have. (Peter)

But when asked whether they liked their new analytical awareness, opinions were divided. Unlike the girls, several of the younger boys (14–15 years of age) favoured the possibilities of emotional distance that this awareness entailed. According to 17-year-old John, however:

you only think about [the film] afterwards. If you haven't noticed all those things [when watching], then it has been a really good one, really absorbing.

He clearly prefers involvement. This difference in evaluation may be rooted in the ambiguity of looking. To look involves the power of gazing at others but also the pleasure of being watched – in Christoph Wulf's cogent term, this is 'the engulfed look' (Wulf, 1984: 24). Video-making allows an experimentation with both these aspects as is evident, for example, in the two boys' improvisation on adverts. Their interaction is an oscillation between active and passive visual power: the cameraman selects specific angles while the actor controls the character presentation. But at the same time his acting is a letting-go, an enjoyment of being a visual object for his friend who responds by a similar involvement in the game.

Looking trains emotional distanciation as well as emotional immersion. Judged within the context of adolescent development, it is understandable that the younger boys prefer the critical gaze harnessing emotionally charged images. That these images often invite an immersion into romance, tenderness, and intimacy are entirely in line with the gender differences already encountered.

One should not underrate the importance of distanciation. In the form of laughs and remarks it may create an emotional shield fending off the impact of excessive violence in the watching of many 'nasties' (my own investigation did not include such films). Distanciation certainly helped some of the more insecure participants in the video group gain a self-assertion that fed back into other situations. Ron said: 'you get a chance of testing yourself, see what you are good at, learn to talk to people, having them say something instead of just "yes" and "no"'. For 'people,' one might read friends in general and girls in particular.

The experience of video production influenced the group's modes of visual reception, just as it trained communicative competences that can be employed in other areas of life. But was it important that these competences had been gained through an *aesthetic* process? Answering this question must necessarily be more speculative. Not only because the personal benefits may not yet be proved because the participants are still too young. But equally because such benefits may not be 'proveable'. By nature, aesthetic production is an experience through all our senses and thus involves more than can be put into words or rational cognition. The aesthetic process is less tangible though not necessarily less important than learning in a narrower sense. This makes the process harder to analyse as well.

Asked if they would pursue their video interest in the future, many in the group acted with surprise ('well, I never thought of this as an option'), and all but one relegated video-making to the marginal, albeit absorbing, area of possible adult hobbies. Their rational rejection of incorporating their aesthetic experiences as important aspects of their future lives contrasted sharply with their undivided attention when talking to me about, and especially making, videos.[11] This tension between conscious limitation and unconscious intensity is of course easy to explain at a surface level: young people know perfectly well that they cannot all be actors, film directors, or video technicians. Their schooling also makes them realize that 'real' training is seldom fun, from which they infer that if you have fun you do not learn anything worthwhile.

To such sociological explanations one may add more psychological reasons for their ambivalence. Aesthetic production is a playful testing ground for 'excessive' behaviour and unrecognized emotions (as Ron said: 'you get a chance of testing yourself, see what you are really good at'). The process allows a negotiation of present problems and wishes along with a projection of future possibilities through an enjoyable regression to the safe patterns of childhood play. Most young people, however, desperately want to grow up, to grow out of their childhood ways. So aesthetic production becomes an inherently contradictory experience: cherished as a safety net of pleasure and dismissed as a constriction to what they perceive to be a 'proper' adult existence. Here, being an expert in falling seems in slight demand.

Only to the degree in which the sensuous experiences of aesthetic production are accepted as integral elements of both male and female identities in adulthood may these processes feed back as a conscious enrichment of adolescence. To the best of my knowledge, this integration is not happening at the moment. Dissolution of local networks and economic rationalizations in the name of modernization and effectivity have not enhanced most adults' possibilities of personal development. The current increase in adolescents' aesthetic production might therefore be seen as a mostly unconscious resistance to disintegration and the narrowing of adult capabilities more than as a sign of widened opportunities for the young.

Aesthetic experiences entail an indirect critique of verbal language and linear reasoning. Through them, we regain what Schutz and Luckmann describe as the *polythetic* qualities of our first perceptions that include all the senses (Schutz and Luckmann, 1974: 119). Young people are ambiguous about these perceptions because they acknowledge the constrictions of existing reality without relinquishing their experiences of wider realities that unite sense and sensibility, work and pleasure. Unlike many of my own generation, who have sought to establish self-contained utopian communities, the middle-class youngsters I have encountered are pragmatics. Aesthetic production, to them, may be an arbiter in the chaos of everyday life, but it is still lodged within its conflicts and contradictions. Whether one speaks as a Marxist stressing youth unemployment and the increasing social pressure on the young in an adverse economic climate, or one emphasizes a post-modern perspective of cultural decentredness, adolescents' aesthetic production develops against the grain of existing constraints. It momentarily suspends social demands through processes that are literally in the hands of the participants controlling its pace and shape. The growth and vitality of these processes reveal that, psychologically speaking, young people may be among the most capable in employing the energies that are also let loose by the complex cultural and social relocations of the 1980s.

Theoretical perspectives

The new media are here to stay. The youthful absorption of videos and other technological novelties are integral to social reality and cultural identities. Pictures *are* thrilling both to watch and to make. As for the latter, I think children and young people should be given wider opportunities to produce pictures and to control the production process themselves. Not for *pedagogical* reasons: as I have indicated, young video-makers do not necessarily become more critical viewers, and if they do they do not always like what they see. Not for *social* reasons: certainly no one in my group was kept off the streets or away from television because of their activities in the youth school: video production is no antidote to the visual bombardment of the professional media. Not for *artistic* reasons: the video group – perhaps because of their age – liked the aesthetic process and its substance more than the finished products and their aesthetic forms, unlike artists to whom form and product are essential qualities of their *oeuvres*; and it remains to be seen whether any of these adolescents will make a career in the visual arts. Aesthetic production in general and visual production in particular should be entertained for their own sake and on their own merits as a widening of our ordinary experiences and sensibilities. It should not be a means to a predefined end. Strange as it may seem, freedom and openness are what in the final analysis make aesthetic production serve other purposes. As my own work suggests, the participants' voluntary engagement is a precondition for their experience of visual pleasure through which the necessary frustrations in the process may be tackled. The aesthetic negotiation is what makes the process unique.

Widening the opportunities of visual production, however, should not establish a hierarchy of visual pleasure. We should hesitate to regard visual production *per se* as a necessarily better, more genuine or creative, activity than visual reception. For by doing so we only perpetuate the standard notions that it is better to read a book than see a film, but that it is even better to *write* a book. To my group, and I think to most young people, aesthetic production and reception, high and low culture, form integral parts of an everyday culture that needs no value judgements to be created and enjoyed. Popular culture forms an important source for their aesthetic imagination whose results feed back into their perceptions of the commercial output.

Seen from the vantage point of the people involved, aesthetic production has some important implications for cultural studies in general and for media studies in particular. We must widen our conception of aesthetics: aesthetic production and reception are mutual aspects in the formation of everyday cultures and should be studied as such. This perspective necessarily challenges the modernist notions of 'high' art as *the* locus of aesthetic production, just as it serves to undermine the elitist dichotomy between aesthetic production and reception.[12] By insisting that we all actively shape and recreate a variety of everyday cultures by employing a varied assemblage of aesthetic forms and conventions, high and low, we may help to redirect the perspective on aesthetics. More important in the present context, we may help to redirect the perspectives of research.

Youth groups have long been very visible cultural catalysts in most western societies, and studies on youth culture have been central to the development of cultural studies in several countries over the last fifteen or twenty years. In British cultural studies, 'style' has been the concept commonly used to analyse, and to critique, a homology between social and cultural levels of youthful expression (Hall and Jefferson, 1976; Hebdige, 1979). Theories of everyday aesthetics, in their emphasis on aesthetics as a *variety of concrete practices*, may further elucidate the diversity of cultural production and reception. More centrally, they may help specify how aesthetics serve contradictory needs for ordinary adolescents, boys and girls. By extending and diversifying the cultural field and by discriminating its uses, the concept of everyday aesthetics may even be an eye-opener to women's private and more hidden cultures that have largely been bypassed by existing investigations (McRobbie, 1980).

Within media studies, the current growth in reception theories suggests that an increasing number of researchers have taken to heart Jay G. Blumler's affirmation that 'the study of mass communication as a process without systematic investigation of audience response is like a sexology that ignores the orgasm' (Blumler, 1980: 373). As one way of overcoming the impassse governing dominant traditions of communication research, reception theories focus on the interaction between texts and recipients. In my view, investigations of people's own media production may prise open for analysis aspects that reception researchers consider essential but which they have difficulties in substantiating analytically. I am thinking, in particular, of the unconscious and semiconscious aspects of media experience which, as my description should have made clear, surface with exceptional clarity through the process of aesthetic creation and which feed on and feed back *into* codes of visual reception. An inclusion of visual production as an element in media research may widen its scope and specify its analyses of visual pleasure.[13]

Importantly, my investigation demonstrates that the interaction between media contents and media users is not only a dynamic and changing relation, it is also a multi-layered and gender-specific process of social signification encompassing both an aesthetic and a socio-psychological level: both we and the media are reinterpreted through the process.[14] Multiple uses require diversified analyses. Along with the familiar stock of semiological and ethnographic methods my own work has benefited from phenomenological theory because of its particular sensitivity to the processual characteristics of immediate experience and interpersonal communication. These characteristics are essential also to in-depth studies of the personal implications of the commercial media flow.

The theories of everyday aesthetics, incorporating both production and reception, are essentially critical theories. Based on an often unacknowledged ideal of a holistic personality, they directly or indirectly critique the priority of abstract rationality and the linearity of language over other modes of perception. This critique makes them essential in clearing the ground for an analytical understanding of *visual* pleasure that is nurtured by non-verbal and semi-conscious sensations. Visual pleasure is, indeed, more than meets the eye.

The emphasis in theories of everyday aesthetics upon the senses as genuine elements in human cognition, their equal insistence upon playfulness and pleasure as ends in themselves, may all seem to put these theories squarely in the postmodern camp at its most populist: the appropriate answers to social chaos and cultural dissolution are individual emotional kicks and an enjoyment in playing the game of illusion. But contrary to such visions of a postmodern free for all, the theories of everyday aesthetics never lose sight of reality and its contradictory production of experience. The theories challenge received notions of rationalist essentialism and monolithic ideological criticism without resorting to cultural relativism or elitist generalizations. Aesthetics remains a concrete element in reality and an essential aspect of everbody's cognition of that reality and ourselves: everyday aesthetics may be a submerged area of analysis. But that does not make it a luxurious or even superfluous detail of daily experience.

Crucially, I think the perspective of everyday aesthetics may re-open a politicized engagement with the important question of *aesthetic value* which the dissolution of the high/low dichotomy has largely left unanswered within both media and cultural studies. If we acknowledge that everyday aesthetics and the production of social relations are aspects of the same process, then it follows that aesthetic value cannot be separated from aesthetic use. The nexus is people's actual needs and experiences, their conscious problems, and unconscious desires: what are those varied and varying experiences? How are these given concrete aesthetic form? What are the implications of these aesthetic creations for the people involved? Making video may not be a more enriching experience than watching *Dynasty* which, in turn, may be as engaging as reading Kafka's *The Process*. All of these activities may be abandoned for a night out with one's friends. The relative value of these cultural processes may be judged only in relation to the different social and sexual needs that they serve.

Practical implications

Research on everyday aesthetics as a critical widening of media and cultural studies becomes particularly pertinent when we see this research in relation to current trends within education and the social services. In Scandinavia, radio, video, and other means of aesthetic expression are becoming hot issues in obvious response to the failure of social and pedagogical practices based on verbal cognition and attitudes of 'we-know-what-is-best-for-you'. Critical teachers and social workers, who actively seek new ways of working with young people, grasp the making of murals, musicials, and media programmes as meaningful activities: the young participants immediately take to them, the aesthetic expressions strengthen their self-worth which in turn may be recycled into other, more marketable, means of training. Within the social services, aesthetic production is used primarily with unemployed adolescents and 'at risk' groups. In schools, media education (analysis and production) occupies an optional, but often important, position in aesthetic activities with young people.

Most aesthetic productions involving young people are a success if judged by the criterion of their active participation. But no one seems to ask if success is a good thing. My own work experiences suggest that asking that question is essential. The apparent aimlessness of the video course was at the heart of its success for the participants, as I have suggested. When aesthetic production is used as an element in social and pedagogical processes, it is vital that the aims of these processes are clarified. So far, the organizers have been very committed and enthusiastic, and the aesthetic experiences have been valuable to adults and adolescents alike. But this may not last. Current technological development, apart from its world-wide political implications, on a more limited scale is likely to foster decisive pedagogical changes in many western societies: individual versatility and collective mobility may become even more important abilities in the struggle for economic survival facing diminishing working populations. How are these personal qualities to be nurtured in the western youth generations that before the year 2000 will decrease by about a third and who know that they are a scarce human resource?

Because of its immediate appeal and its creative potential, aesthetic production could well come to play a key role in the attempts to answer this intricate question. If so, then there is a real danger that adolescents' aesthetic activities – which now operate as important physical and mental breathing spaces – will be co-opted as a handy pedagogical tool that is all the more effective because it is more subtle. Rather than telling young people what to do, we let them do what they want and then judge them by their results. The outcome of such an approach may very likely be either the participants' rejection of these activities or an acceptance of them as superfluous entertainment.

More research is not going to resolve these complex problems. Still, researchers are agents in the process. Speaking from the limited perspective of video production, I find it important to stress that aesthetic production is not a value-free method of teaching, it is an attitude to learning covering a specific commitment and attitude to life. Used as a generalized and instrumental method applicable without these commitments and attitudes, aesthetic production loses its importance. The problem is to find a balance between voluntary and open processes and continuity of social and pedagogical goals.

Video is an obvious choice for aesthetic production: it is relatively cheap, easy to handle, and its novelty makes it escape the cultural biases that many young people entertain in relation to more traditional forms of aesthetic expression such as drama and drawing. These are either regarded as childish pursuits or as activities enjoyed only by a minority of weird artists and culture snobs. Video production, then, could become an important catalyst to cultural rejuvenations within education and social work. But the point of departure must be the visual practices, not pedagogical or social problems. Both researchers and practitioners must describe what video does in an aesthetic sense before we decide what it should do in a social sense.

This relation between contents and contexts may be particularly relevant within a gender perspective. Everyday aesthetics has traditionally been relegated to the female sphere: home furnishing, knitting, and generally adding the aesthetic airs and graces have long been regarded as proper feminine pursuits. It may therefore come as no surprise that girls are often keen participants in the aesthetic processes of adolescence. What is more remarkable is that girls, at least middle-class girls, increasingly transcend the home and the family with which feminine aesthetics is so closely associated. Their everyday aesthetics is shaped and performed in the streets and other public arenas traditionally dominated by boys and men. Whether the girls attend dance courses, go training on their rollerskates, or rehearse a rock musical, they widen the female space and their own presence in it.

Similarly, the growth in aesthetic production enjoyed by young people implies a widening of boys' experiences. Even if many still opt for the most physical and/or technical activities such as motorcross riding and home computing, boys' increasing engagement with music and media, for instance, nevertheless signals an unprecedented openness to explore areas of experience beyond narrow conceptions of masculinity.

Aesthetic reorientations do not spell social or gender realignments in a wider sense: they are still mainly middle-class phenomena. Even so, they indicate how everyday aesthetics may serve different needs: for boys, the widening of aesthetic contents may be the most important challenge to traditional masculine roles, while for girls, the contexts of aesthetic production may prove the most decisive. For adults and adolescents alike, the new media are going to change our perceptions in an aesthetic as well as a social sense. If postmodernists have tended to interpret this change as a replacement of the Cartesian dictum *cogito ergo sum* by a *video ergo sum*, I suggest that we start acting on the basis of *video ergo cogito*.

University of Copenhagen, Denmark

Proper names in the article have been changed. All translations are by the author if not otherwise indicated.

Notes

1 Video reception encompasses a range of media types and viewing situations. Most important for young people in Scandinavia are rented video cassettes watched together with peers, and satellite television, dominated by pop videos and watched more individually, such as Sky Channel, Super Channel and Scan-Sat/TV-3. Access to video, whether through cable or cassette, generally enhances viewing time, particularly for boys in their early teens. See Danmedia (1984); Filipson and Schyller (1982); Montén (1988).

2 Within a Scandinavian context, Sweden has witnessed the clearest government proposals to curb video violence. See Våldsskildringsutredningen (1987, 1988); and critique of the debate in Roe (1985).

3 Finland and Iceland already have commercial television. In Denmark, the challenge from satellites and foreign commercial channels has spurred the introduction by the Danish government of a second, commercial and state-subsidized, channel modelled on the British Channel 4 and opening in October 1988. In summer 1988 the Norwegian government made proposals for the introduction of commercials on the public television channel: profits should go to the financing of a second national channel from 1993. So far, the Swedish public-service system retains its two non-commercial channels.

4 In Denmark, there are currently about ten media centres aimed specifically at children and young people (about 1 million in all) and offering a variety of technical facilities as well as practical advice.

5 This work was part of a larger project on the gender-specific role played by aesthetic production in adolescence in general and Danish youth culture in particular.

6 The boys' imitation of these films correspond to their actual pattern of reception. In both the film and video markets in Denmark, British and American productions make up 75 per cent of the total output. Only 15 per cent of titles are

Danish, and all of these are subsidized by public funding. (Schmidt, 1987: 50, 52).

7 Paying attention to details has traditionally been regarded as a characteristic of women (Schor, 1987). My project (see note 5) indicates that at least in adolescence boys as well as girls take pleasure in details, both in a literal and a symbolic sense. They differ, however, in their use of details, girls often stressing the working together of details to form a whole (cf. their interest in a realistic plot) and boys emphasizing the single details or the heterogeneity in their appearance.

8 For a detailed critique, see Hartwig (1976).

9 Schutz's definition is used here about the level of reality as it *appears* to us. Although few scholars today would embrace his insistence upon primordial, direct, or spontaneous experiences, Schutz's theories may nevertheless help us explore the various ways in which we naturalize most experiences as a routinized basis of our everyday lives. Such an exploration may be of particular relevance at a time when many critics are busy deconstructing modern reality without paying much attention to its various forms of expression and their varying significance to people.

10 Lodging aesthetics within the contradictions of real experience makes these theories different from philosophical studies defining everyday aesthetics as a specific 'organising place, "above" particular concerns' (Kupfer, 1983: 6).

11 The contradiction between conscious and unconscious evaluation of video production could only surface because I not only interviewed the group members about their activities, but I also followed the actual production *process*. This dual approach gave me more opportunities to analyse different levels of experience and their incongruities than is possible with the in-depth interviews normally employed in qualitative media research.

12 Recent studies in Britain and the United States on the crossover between art and popular culture substantiate the infelicity of the high/low dichotomy to cultural research (MacCabe, 1986; Walker, 1987). Still, these investigations keep firmly within professional aesthetic boundaries, be it car design or record sleeves, and in that respect they are in perfect accord with both modernists and post-modernists in their neglect of the more elusive processes involved in everyday aesthetics.

13 Investigations of ordinary people's visual productions may perhaps even elucidate the aesthetic processes that are involved in the creation of commercial products. Rational calculation is still not enough to make a box office hit or a number one rating.

14 This process of mutual interpretation and reinterpretation is best seen in a longer historical perspective. For a theoretical discussion of this process and an empirical substantiation of its results, see Drotner (1988).

References

Blos, Peter (1962) *On Adolescence: A Psychoanalytic Interpretation*. New York, London: Free Press/Collier-Macmillan.

Blumler, Jay G. (1980) 'Mass communication research in Europe: some origins and perspectives'. *Media, Culture and Society*, 2 (1): 367–76.

Criegern, Axel von (ed.) (1982) *Handbuch der ästhetischen Erziehung*. Stuttgart: Kohlhammer.

Danmedia (1984) *Video i danske hjem. Rapport nr. 6* [Video in Danish homes. Report no. 6]. Copenhagen: Danmedia.

Drotner, Kirsten (1988) *English Children and Their Magazines 1751–1945*. New Haven and London: Yale University Press.

Ehmer, Hermann K. (ed.) (1979) *Ästhetische Erziehung und Alltag*. Lahn-Giessen: Anabas.

Filipson, Leni and Schyller, Ingela (1982) *Tv- och videotittande bland barn och ungdom. PUB rapport nr. 20* [Children's and Adolescents' Television and Video Uses. Audience and Programme Research Dept. Report no. 20]. Stockholm: Swedish Broadcasting Corporation.

Glogauer, W. (1988) *Videofilm-Konsum der Kinder und Jugendlichen: Erkenntnisstand und Wirkungen*. Bad Heilbrunn: Klinkhart.

Hall, Stuart and Jefferson, Tony (eds) (1976) *Resistance Through Rituals: Youth Subcultures in Post-War Britain*. London: Hutchinson/CCCS.

Halloran, James and Jones, Marcia (1985) *Learning about the Media: Media Education and Communication Research*. Paris: UNESCO.

Hartwig, Helmut (1976) 'Sehen lernen: Bildgebrauch und Zeichnen – Historische Rekonstruktion und didaktische Perspektiven', in his *Sehen lernen: Kritik und Weiterarbeit am Konzept 'Visuelle Kommunikation'*. Cologne: DuMont Schauberg.

—— (1980) *Jugendkultur: ästhetische Praxis in der Pubertät*. Reinbek: Rowohlt.

Hebdige, Dick (1979) *Subculture: the Meaning of Style*. London: Methuen.

Heller, Agnes and Fehér, Ferenc (eds) (1986) *Reconstructing Aesthetics: Writings of the Budapest School*. Oxford: Blackwell.

Kupfer, Joseph (1983) *Experience as Art: Aesthetics in Everyday Life*. Albany: State University of New York Press.

Lefebvre, Henri (1971) *Everyday Life in the Modern World*. Trans. Sacha Rabinovitch. New York and London: Harper & Row. (Originally published 1968.)

MacCabe, Colin (ed.) (1986) *High Theory/Low Culture: Analysing Popular Television and Film*. Manchester: Manchester University Press.

McRobbie, Angela (1980) 'Settling accounts with subculture: a feminist critique'. *Screen Education*, 34: 37–49.

Masterman, Len (1985) *Teaching the Media*. London: Comedia.

Montén, Richard (1988) *Tv-tittandet i svensk kabel-tv-områden, mars* 1987. *PUB rapport nr. 11* [Television Use in Swedish Cable Television Areas. Audience and Programme Research Dept. Report no. 11]. Stockholm: Swedish Broadcasting Corporation.

Nibbrig, Christiaan L. Hart (1978) *Ästhetik: Materialen zu ihrer Geschichte*. Frankfurt/M: Suhrkamp.

Otto, Britta (1984) *Untersuchungen zum Paradigmenwechsel in der ästhetischen Erziehung*. Frankfurt/M: Peter Lang.

Roe, Keith and Salmonsen, Karin (1983) *The Uses and Effects of Video Viewing among Swedish Adolescents. Media Panel Report no. 31*. Lund: Dept. of Sociology, University of Lund.

Roe, Keith (1985) 'The Swedish moral panic over video, 1980–1984'. *Nordicom-Information*, 2–3: 13–18.

Schmidt, Kaare (1987) 'Et åbent vindue' [An open window]. In Witt, Gunnar (ed.) *Video et ungt medie – de unges medie* [Video: A Young Medium – medium of the young]. Copenhagen: Unge Pædagoger: 5–60.

Schor, Naomi (1987) *Reading in Detail: Aesthetics and the Feminine*. London and New York: Methuen.

Schutz, Alfred (1972) *The Phenomenology of the Social World*. Trans. and ed. George Walsh and Frederick Lehnert. London: Heinemann. (Originally published 1932.)

Schutz, Alfred and Luckmann, Thomas (1974) *The Structures of the Life World*. Trans. Richard M. Zaner and H. Tristram Engelhardt. London: Heinemann.

Våldsskildringsutredningen (1987, 1988) *Videovold. I, II* [Video Violence. I, II]. Stockholm: Almänna förlaget.

Walker, John A. (1987) *Cross-Overs: Art into Pop/Pop into Art*. London: Methuen/Comedia.

Wulf, Christoph (1984) 'Das gefährdete Auge: ein Kaleidoskop der Geschichte des Sehens', in Dietmar Kamper and Christoph Wulf (eds) *Das Schwinden der Sinne*. Frankfurt: Suhrkamp.

MARIE GILLESPIE

TECHNOLOGY AND TRADITION: AUDIO-VISUAL CULTURE AMONG SOUTH ASIAN FAMILIES IN WEST LONDON

Introduction

T his ethnographic account is based on research among south Asian families in Southall, Middlesex.[1] Southall is a 'town', formerly an autonomous London borough, with a population of some 65,000. Its demographic majority is of south Asian origin, predominantly of Sikh religion, but divided along cross-cutting cleavages of national, regional, religious, and caste heritage.

The study evolved over seven years of teaching in two Southall high schools where the popularity of 'Indian' films was evident; and yet various manifestations of resistance to its pleasures seemed to signify a great deal more than mere expressions of taste or preference.

The extensive use of the VCR at home to view 'Indian'[2] films represents a powerful means for grandparents and parents to maintain links with their country of origin. Second-generation children, however, born and educated in Britain, position themselves and are positioned rather differently in relation to notions of 'Asian' and 'British' culture. The legitimation of state racism in postwar Britain has been secured in an important way around particular ideological constructions of south Asian cultures, especially their marriage and family systems. For long, these have been seen to be based on archaic and traditional customs and practices and are presented as an 'alien threat' to the 'British way of life'. But in much of the literature produced by the 'Race Relations Industry' it is 'culture-clash' and inter-generational conflict, low self-esteem and negative self-image, rather than racism, that, paradoxically, have been identified as both 'the problem' and 'the cause'.[3]

Such dominant assumptions went unchallenged as young Asian voices were usually excluded or marginalized from debates which concerned them. This paper therefore is an attempt to re-present 'their voices', concentrating on their interpretations of popular Indian films and the themes and issues arising from their viewing experiences and which they find salient.

The ethnographic data are based on interviews carried out with young people predominantly of Panjabi origin and aged 15–18. A set of basic questions was used to spark off each interview. When do you watch? What do you watch? With whom do you watch? Who chooses what you watch in which situations? The wide range of methodological issues which the study raises will not be dealt with here, and this account will be structured around four main concerns:

First, it will contextualize the study by briefly outlining the history of Indian cinema in Southall, and the shift from public exhibition to private viewing in the home, secondly, it will examine the implications of this shift by focusing on the family-viewing context. It will explore questions of choice and preference alongside issues of family power and control. The third part will examine the responses of young people to Indian films and the factors mediating their various interpretations. Finally, it will bring together the diverse strands of the study in order to highlight the different ways in which viewing experiences are used.

Indian cinema in Southall: from public pleasure to private leisure

The first 'Indian' films were shown in Southall in 1953 in hired halls and then in three local cinemas. During the 1960s and 1970s the cinema provided the principal weekend leisure activity in Southall and represented an occasion for families and friends to get together; the social event of the week.

In 1978, when VCRs came on the market, many families were quick to seize the opportunity to extend their choice and control over viewing in the home. Many Asian communities obtained them as early as 1978/9 before most other households in Britain. It is now estimated that between 40 and 50 per cent of households in Britain now own or rent a VCR but in Southall the figure is held to be 80 per cent.[4]

Most shops rent popular Hindi (also known as 'Bombay') films and although films in Panjabi and Urdu are also obtainable from shops they lack the broad-based appeal of the popular Hindi movie. In fact the Bombay film has gained something of a cultural hegemony in south Asia and among many 'Asian' settlers across the world. To understand this one has to look to the specific evolution of the popular Hindi genre which, in order to appeal to a mass audience, had to produce films which would cross the linguistic, religious, and regional differences that exist within India, as indeed within Southall.

Many of the films combine a catholicity or universality of appeal with a careful handling of regional and religious differences. A distinctive form of Bombay Hindi, characterized by a certain 'linguistic openness' has evolved which makes most films accessible also to speakers of other south Asian languages. The distinctive visual style, often foregrounded over dialogue, combines with successive modes of spectacle, action and emotion which facilitates cross-cultural understanding.[5] In the light of this we can understand the huge uptake of Hindi films on cassette among the diverse linguistic groups in Southall.

With the arrival of video, the adventure, romance, and drama of the Bombay film was to be enjoyed in domestic privacy. A small piece of home technology brought the cinema hall into the home, or so it appeared. A lot was gained but much was lost. The weekly outing became a thing of the past as the cinemas closed and the big screen image shrunk into the TV box and entered the flow of everyday life in the living room.

In Southall the rapid expansion of the home video market needs to be considered not only as providing an extension to an already important and dynamic film culture but also very much a response on the part of a black community to life in Britain. Southall, like many other black communities, has come into existence in the first instance as a result of racist immigration and housing policies. Such communities have developed as 'sanctuaries' against the racism they experience.[6] The exclusion and marginalization of many people in Southall from mainstream British society, coupled with the failure to provide adequate leisure/culture facilities, has (like among the *Gastarbeiter* (guest worker) Turkish community in West Germany) contributed to the development of an important home video culture.

But the consequences of a decade of video use are perceived in contradictory ways by the youth of Southall. Many young people feel that the VCR has served further to isolate the community from mainstream British society. It is also seen to have specific effects on the lives of women: 'The video has isolated the community even more. They might as well be in India, especially the women.' Others see it as a liberating pleasure, especially for females: 'Some girls can't get out of the house that much so they can get a film and keep themselves occupied within the four walls of the house. It's an advantage for them.'

Such contradictory evaluations need to be seen in the contexts in which they originate.

Domestic viewing contexts

During the course of the study it became possible to construct a broad typology of contexts and associated texts. For the purpose of this account I shall concentrate on weekend family viewing because this situation was so frequently and consistently discussed by all interviewees, and due to the importance given to it within this cultural context.[7]

The VCR is used predominantly at the weekend in most families. Viewing 'Indian' films on video is the principal, regular family leisure activity. Weekend family gatherings around the TV set is a social ritual repeated in many families. The VCR and TV screen become the focus and locus of interaction. Notions of togetherness and communality are stressed: 'It's probably the only time in the week that we are all together so when we're watching a film at least we're all together.'

This togetherness is by no means that of passive viewers: 'No one is silent, we're all talking through the film about what's happening here and there and generally having a chat . . . it sort of brings you closer together.'

The weaving of conversation through the narrative is facilitated by an impressive familiarity with films brought about by repeated viewings. The episodic structure of films which moves the spectator through the different modes of spectacle, song and dance, drama, action, and affect also provides natural breaks for talk, emotion and reflection.

With such large family gatherings the question of power and control over viewing becomes important. The interviews highlight the way in which parents actively set and maintain viewing rules which govern viewing patterns and modes of parent–child interaction.

While the father is usually seen to determine when children are allowed access to the screen by his absence or presence in the home, the mother is perceived as exercising a greater degree of power and control over the choice of what is watched. This was a significant pattern across the interviews, emphasizing the important role mothers play in socializing their children in the domestic context. It also makes clear that the relationship between family power structures and family viewing patterns is not one of simple correspondence.

There are also clear differences in the attentiveness and in the degree of salience of Indian films to various family members, which are obscured by the simple observation that the family all watched the same programme.[8] Many young people say they sit with parents and view parts of the films just to please them or that their parents encourage or even 'force' them to watch.

As gender differences are important to understand parental control over viewing they are also a significant factor in understanding young people's viewing preferences and behaviour. Boys tend to experience greater freedom in deciding how they use their leisure time and spend more time engaged in activities outside the home. In contrast, girls are usually socialized to remain within the domestic realm and often participate in strong and supportive female cultures in the home where the viewing of Indian films on video frequently plays an important role. This explains to some extent the generally greater engagement with popular Hindi videos on the part of most girls interviewed. In one interview two boys rather begrudgingly claim: 'It doesn't hurt to watch an Indian film with the parents.' 'No, it kills you.'

In spite of this repeatedly expressed reluctance the way in which the screen can serve social interaction in the family tends to override individual preferences and return young people to the family situation. One boy commented to the general agreement of the group: 'Well we don't usually stay in another room while they're watching, if you've got something to yourself, you isolate yourself don't you?' It is clear that what might be seen on the one hand as 'enforced' or 'reluctant' viewing can take on pleasurable connotations where the emphasis is on 'being together'. Parents do not have much time for leisure due to long working hours and shift work, so the time when the family is together around the TV set is often much appreciated by all concerned.

Conversely, the family audience is frequently fragmented by English and American films: 'When it's Indian films it's all of us together but when it's English films it's just me and my brother.' This fragmentation is partly due to the texts of English and American films themselves. Given parental reservations about the language, sensuality, and references to sexuality, young people may often prefer to view them on their own to escape parental censure or vigilance.

You may now have the impression that the avid consumption of VCR films falls into two neat categories. While Hindi films tend to be viewed in large family gatherings and to be celebrated by intense social interaction, British and American films tend to be consumed on their own in a more or less assertive circumvention of parental control and preferences. While viewing patterns tend indeed to correspond to this dichotomy, young people's viewing of Hindi films raises further ethnographic questions about perceptions of 'Indianness' and Britain or India and 'Britishness'.

Representations of India

For young people in Southall who have little or no direct experience outside the UK, perceptions of India will be founded on a complex combination of factors. But invariably they will also be influenced by 'Indian' films. Even for those who have lived or spent long periods in India the films provide a counterpoint to their own personal experiences.

Throughout the interviews a series of related binary oppositions frame and structure accounts of how India is perceived through the films:

  Village.................................City
  Poverty..............................Wealth
  Communality.....................Individualism
  Tradition.............................Modernity
  Morality..............................Vice

The interviewees' accounts are in some measure reconstructions of and responses to patterned social and moral discourses prevalent in popular Hindi films, where a pristine and moral rural India is often constructed by opposing it to an exotic and decadent 'other' – usually signified by symbols of the west and city life.

Thus, across the interviews, village life is frequently contrasted with city life. The village community is seen as one of extended kin where co-operation and communality prevail, notions of individualism are absent. Village life is seen as 'pure' because 'people are so honest there, they never look with the "evil eye", they help each other even though they're poor, they never "skank" [betray] one another'.

Such interpretations contrast with those of city life which, through the films, is perceived as decadent, immoral, and polluted – a place 'where prostitutes hang out and where even pundits [priests] try to rape girls'.

There was considerable criticism of the 'unrealistic' portrayal of village life and an often acute awareness is shown of the selective and ideological nature of representations: 'There's not so much about the landless labourers and the position of women, you know, who spend hours and hours looking for water and fuel . . . in the scorching heat.'

Exploitation of the poor by the rich is another common theme and the plight of the illiterate landless labourers was referred to on several occasions: 'The films show how rich treat poor, how they don't go to school and have to work from when very young, they can't read and so rich people trick them and take their land and crops.'

Striking gender differences emerge in the framing of accounts. Girls often express their perceptions of India through an exploration of the social and moral values inherent in the films via a 'retelling' of the narratives. In contrast boys seem to be much more concerned with representational issues, particularly 'negative images' and, in many cases, reject Hindi films *per se* on that basis.

Several male respondents see Indian films as offensive in their emphasis on poverty and corruption: 'They should not portray India as if it's really poor and backward even though they're Indians themselves, it's degrading; that's a lot of the reason I don't like Indian films.'

Others ridicule the 'backward image' of 'Indians' in the films because of the different norms associated with fashion and style but they also remark upon the selective nature of images: 'they follow up too late in India, they still wear flares, though I must admit they're not backward in everything they're very advanced in technology but they don't show you those aspects of India'. One boy vehemently rejected the films and wished to dissociate himself from both films and India but not without some irony: 'I didn't learn anything from the films apart from the fact that India is one of the most corrupt countries in the world', and later, 'that country has nothing to do with me any more'.

Such discussions often provoke comments on representations of India in British media more generally which is seen on the whole to reinforce an 'uncivilized', poverty-stricken image of India: 'Documentaries shown in this country degrade India badly as well.' Strong resentment is expressed at the way India is 'degraded' in the west by the circulation of images of poverty, underdevelopment, death, and disease. Such images are linked to the 'degradation' of Indians in Britain where they 'get racist harassment'.

In identifying 'salient' themes and making selective interpretations, a range of 'meanings' are projected onto the films which undoubtedly derive from experiences of racism in Britain. Such experiences underpin and sensitize responses to constructions of Indian society in Hindi films and in the media generally. Boys, in particular, show an understanding of how Indian films may be rebuked and ridiculed as 'backward', 'foreign' and 'ludicrous' by 'outsiders' (for example their white peers) but they also, clearly, feel somewhat estranged from the sense of 'Indianness' and from the 'India' represented in the films. At the same time, there is a tacit acknowledgement that the films may be used to confirm what constitute dominant discourses on India in British society, and an underlying awareness of how they function as racist discourses. As a result the boys would appear to occupy shifting and often contradictory positions from which they view and interpret the films – positions which vary according to context.

It would appear that experiences of racism as well as the reading of films are gender specific. A similar connection may be detected between gender and genre.

Genre

For nearly a century Hindi films have been either rebuked or ignored in the west by critics, academics, and film enthusiasts alike. Such institutionalized disdain and ignorance is not only a symptom of racism but feeds directly into it. The fierce rejection of the popular Hindi film, seen as a genre in itself, especially among the boys interviewed, echoes western critical discourses about the genre. Films are consistently criticized for being 'all the same', based on 'ideas got from Westerns . . . just a mixture of everything . . . commercial . . . full of songs and running round trees and rose gardens'.

An 18-year-old male interviewee in a rather eloquent condemnation of Indian films claims: 'With the standards of media appreciation in the west it's hard to understand the sort of psyche that would appreciate these kinds of film again and again and again. . . . If you've been exposed to a film culture based on plots and detailed cinematography then you'd expect the same from the other culture and if it doesn't match up to that standard you don't want to see it anymore . . . it's like driving a Morris Minor after you've driven a Porsche'.

The widespread condemnation of popular Indian films and the coincidence of views held by both film critics and many of the boys interviewed does not confirm a 'truth' about Hindi cinema but, rather, exposes a common frame of reference which is based on dominant Hollywood and western film-making practices. Clearly, a cultural experience dominated by western film genres will initially militate against an engagement with popular Hindi films, which are likely to disorientate the spectator by subverting generic conventions, even where language presents no barrier.

The focus of this study on south Asian families should not exclude consideration of the context of power relations in which this community lives and between western and 'Third World' countries and cultures. It should, rather, lead us further to consider the nature of white norms and white cultural practices, especially when they entail the abrogation of measures for culturally distinct genres which are clearly incommensurate. Otherwise such a study becomes merely a descriptive exercise, devoid of political responsibility, intent, or analysis.

What becomes clear from the interviews is that for those who do find pleasure in popular Hindi films, the skilful blending of certain generic ingredients is crucial: the screenplay, the music and songs, the emotional appeal, spectacle, production values, and, of course, the stars. But it is above all when narrative is discussed in the interviews that one becomes aware of a deeper engagement with the films. The pleasures involved become apparent but we can also begin to unravel some further causes of resistance to films.

Narrative

According to many writers, the popular Hindi film has evolved from village traditions of epic narration, and the dramas and characters, as well as the structure of the mythological epics, are regularly and openly drawn upon. Film-makers and theorists claim that there are only two stories or 'metatexts', the *Mahabharata* and the *Ramayana*, and that every film can be traced back to these stories.

Vijay Mishra (1985), sees Bombay films as transformations of the narrative structures that may be discovered in these epics. According to him their influence is not limited to narrative form alone since 'these epics were also ideological tools for the expansion of beliefs endorsed by the ruling classes'. In his view the Bombay film legitimates its own existence through a reinscription of its values into those of the *Mahabharata* and the *Ramayana*.

But what seems to distinguish the Hindi film most from its western counterparts is the form and movement of the narrative. The balance between narrative development, spectacle, and emotion is rather different from that in western films. Spectacle alone risks losing an audience. Skilled narration involves the swift transition between well-balanced modes of spectacle and an emotional involvement invited by the reassuring familiarity of many narratives, structured by discourses, deeply rooted in Indian social, moral, and psychic life (Thomas, 1985).

One of the most common assertions across the interviews is that the films all have the same type of stories. Usually this means that the films are 'totally predictable' and therefore not worth watching: 'who wants to sit and watch a film where you can work out the whole plot in the first five minutes?'

Three basic narrative themes of Hindi cinema particularly popular in the late 1970s and 1980s are repeatedly identified and referred to by inter-viewees: (1) 'Dostana', where the bond of male friendship overcomes the desire for a woman; (2) 'lost and found' parents and children are separated and reunited years later following the revelation of mistaken identities; and (3) revenge, villains get their just deserts at the hands of the heroes they wronged.

Interviewees frame their accounts with references to the discourses which commonly structure these narratives, which are those of kinship duty, social obligation, solidarity, respect or 'izzat', and trust. A sense of social 'order' and 'ideal social relations' is related to living in harmony with fate and respecting social obligations and ties of friendship and family.

Hindi film aesthetics, it is argued, are based not on cognition, as in the west, but in re-cognition. Like Hindu epics whose familiar stories form part of the fundamental myths of Indian society, the Hindi film is said to have evolved a broad framework of its own. Anil Saari (1985) claims: 'thus one film is like another, each film confirms once again the world as it is and has been and is likely to remain. The very hopelessness created by poverty and social immobility demands that the world and distractions from it remain as they are. That is indeed how the world is for the average Indian who is not a member of the ruling elite'.

Many interviewees analyse the narrative closure of contemporary Hindi films and compare them with the older, black and white, social-realist films prevalent in the 1950s and 1960s, in which there is an upsurge of renewed interest among young and old alike: 'They all have happy endings by the way . . . unlike the older films, tragedies are being solved by lucky, fortunate events that turn everything upside down, if a heroine's about to die these days she's saved by a handsome doctor at the last moment . . . everything turns out all right and people have nothing to think about, nothing to cry about, unlike the older films'.

Certain fundamental differences in the narrative structures of 'Hindi' and 'western' films are highlighted in the interviews. English films are seen as 'continuous all the way . . . they just continue, no songs, no dances . . . that's why I find them boring'. Pleasure is taken in the non-linear narratives. The intricate and convoluted nature of story-telling becomes apparent through attempts at narrative reconstructions. Hindi films are not tightly linear but build in more or less circular fashion through a number of climaxes which are counterposed with scenes of humour, spectacle, and 'pure' emotional import. It is not so much a question of *what* will happen next that drives the narrative but of *how* it will be framed, not so much an enigma to be solved as a moral disordering to be resolved.

Affective involvement is a crucial component of films and is ensured not only by cinematic techniques which encourage identification and involvement, e.g. the use of close-ups, subjective point of view shots, shot reverse shots, but also through the songs: 'The songs back up everything . . . they have real feeling in them and it's not just any old songs, they relate to the actual situations of the films, they get you emotionally involved and influence you.' As in melodrama, undischarged emotion which cannot be accommodated within the action is expressed in song and music: 'Whenever that song comes on I cry, I can't control myself . . . it's the father of a girl singing to her before she leaves the family to get married, he sings about how you are leaving us now and saying how when you were young I used to hold you in my arms, how I used to play with you. . . . I can't listen to that song without tears pouring out . . . and I think of my sister when she will be leaving us.'

This passage highlights the way in which the Hindi film tends to address and move its spectator by way of affect. This positioning depends for its full effect on certain kinds of cultural competence, most notably a knowledge of the 'ideal moral universe' of the Hindi film. Such cultural knowledge is acquired by young people to very varying degrees and while clearly lending enormous spectator power to some, disallows others from any deep engagement with the films. Conventions of verisimilitude also affect the relationship between text and viewer.

Fantasy and realism

'When I watch an Indian film after that I'm in heaven but I don't relate to the real world like I did . . . they're in rose gardens and the music just springs up from nowhere . . . that's why people like watching them to get away from their own lives, what do drugs do? They take you to another world . . . so do Indian films but they are a safer way out of your problems.'

For those who enjoy Hindi films fantasy is a chief source of pleasure. The songs and dances as well as their settings often provide discrete dream-like sequences and 'a moment of escape from reality' for the spectator. In comparing drug-induced euphoria with the sensations provoked by the fantasy sequences in films this young girl gives us some insight into the desire provoked by the fantasy films: 'I wouldn't mind sitting around in rose gardens or deserts being loved and things like that'.

Such anti-realism is seen by some as escapist: 'They're fantasies for the poor they show them what they cannot afford . . . they're satisfied with the songs . . . they create the dream sequences for them'. They are also seen as exploitative and politically reactionary: 'Most of them are just sheer escapism. . . . I think that has quite a negative effect because it allows people to ignore the reality of their situation, the political realities of India, the exploitation and oppression of the masses'. Several interviewees compared Hindi films of the 1970s and 1980s to the 'social realist' films of the 1950s: 'I think people could identify their immediate lives with them, they were true to life, if they showed a farmer losing his crops after years of hard labour that was a reflection of life and that used to happen to people and they would sit in the cinema and say "well that's true!" There was nothing magical about it as it is now. After this period, people didn't want tragedies, they wanted fantasies, they wanted a means of escape, they wanted to break out of reality and that's when the "masala" films started coming out.'

However, in spite of such criticisms, many of the interviewees do not ignore the cathartic and therapeutic aspects of films. Indeed they are seen to enable a temporary release from the tensions of everyday life and to help discharge distressful emotions: 'I must admit I'm scared of my parents (finding out I have a boyfriend) but after I've watched a film, and listened to a few songs and calmed myself down, I'm not scared of my parents anymore so they give you courage in a way.'

Selective but contradictory judgements about conventions of realism in films are frequent across the interviews as with this girl who on the one hand claims: 'Indian films don't really relate to reality, they're really sheltered . . . it's just fantasy they make it out so perfect'. And yet, later the film's realistic portrayal of love is endorsed: 'Sometimes we'll just sit there and wonder if there's a thing called love . . . whereas in an Indian film you're so convinced that love is real . . . that it's true, that it's really there'.

It is clear that an exposure to western conventions of realism influence responses considerably. Attention is paid to *mise-en-scène* and anachronism is not easily tolerated. A determined fidelity to details of period representation and dress is adhered to by young male respondents: 'They'll show a man fighting for Independence and you'll see a man on a motorbike with sunglasses and jeans they should at least have the clothes of the period'.

'They'll be showing a scene in the eighteenth century with horse-drawn carriage and at the back you'll see 1980s taxis, scooters, and high-rise buildings. It spoils everything. If only they [the directors] thought more about what they were doing, it looks as though they haven't planned it'. Western conventions of realism also provide expectations about the way characters should behave, dress, and act. The reality status of stunt sequences is rebuked where production values are low: 'It's stupid motorbikes crossing lakes when you know it's a cartoon'.

There is in Hindi films an acceptable realism and logic beyond the material which is unbelievable. In fact the criteria of verisimilitude in Hindi cinema appears to refer primarily to the skill demonstrated in manipulating the rules of the film's moral universe. Among regular viewers one is more likely to hear accusations of unbelievability if the codes of ideal kinship are flouted than if the hero performs some outrageously unrealistic feat as is the case with disaffected viewers. In order to acquire a better understanding of the conventions of realism/anti-realism in Hindi cinema one would need to consider much wider issues including concepts and conventions of realism in Indian culture generally. Furthermore, a more detailed study of the important influence of the mythological film genre, essentially moral tales, might shed light on the anti-realist strategies of Bombay cinema.

Social and cultural uses of viewing experiences

The final part of this account concerns the social and cultural uses of viewing experiences, broadening the scope beyond that of contemporary popular Hindi films to include the full range of films viewed.

For the older members of the community, nostalgia is a key element in the pleasure experienced through film. In one particularly moving account by a man in his 70s, tears welled in his eyes as he recounted: 'When we see black-and-white films it reminds us of our childhood, our school days, our school mates, of what we were thinking, of what we did do, of our heroes . . . and I tell you this gives us great pleasure.' The films would appear to act as a form of collective popular memory and some parents are able to convey a sense of their past in India to their children.

With the emergence of second-generation children parents and grand-parents have found new uses for films. These uses are primarily defined in terms of linguistic, religious, and socio-cultural learning. In viewing Indian films together many families are enabled to come together on a 'shared' linguistic basis. Both parents and children see this as a major advantage of watching films: 'They help children get a hold of the language.'

For many children the films provide one of the rare opportunities, outside communication in the family and community, to hear that language used and legitimated: 'They can hear and see how the language is used and should be used'. One boy put it more directly: 'They teach not only the language but how "to be" in an Indian environment.' The notion of language as transmitter of culture is prevalent among parents: 'If the children don't speak the language they lose their culture. Language is a potent symbol of collective identity and often the site of fierce loyalities and emotional power. In the context of a society which constructs linguistic difference as a problem rather than as a tool, the desire to defend and maintain one's linguistic heritage becomes strong.

In a community faced with religious distinctiveness and at times division, it is not surprising that cultural identity is often construed as being based not only on linguistic but also on religious continuity. 'Religious' or mythological films are also watched for devotional purposes, particularly by Hindu families, and often integrated with daily acts of worship: 'When we start fasting we always watch these films, sometimes five times a day . . . you kind of pray to God at the same time you know'.

The films are also used as a form of religious education: 'They help parents teach their children about the Holy Books like the *Ramayana*, the *Mahabharat*, and the *Bhaghavat Gita*. It's the tradition in families to tell the young children the stories but some families don't have the time and so there are children who don't know who is Rama.' In some families viewing devotional films has come to replace reading the holy books. Certainly, the video is seen as a great advantage in familiarizing children with parables and religious stories, largely due to the widespread illiteracy of second- and third-generation children in their mother tongue. Not only are the religious and moral values inherent in the films an important aspect of viewing but the visual representation of the deity plays an extremely important symbolic role in the devotional and ritual acts of worship. This relates to the importance of popular forms of religious iconography in Indian society.

Parents use the films to talk about religious festivals: 'Here we can never really celebrate festivals like Holi which involves the whole village and people smearing each other's faces with colour. No one does that here but when you watch you can really appreciate what it's like in India. Here the kids just know about the fireworks but they don't know the real basic thing about why, they don't know about the religious aspects of the festivals.'

Young people and their parents use the films to negotiate, argue, and agree about a wider range of customs, traditions, values, and beliefs. Together, they often enjoy films which encourage discussion: 'films which bring out the contradictions in families, the arranged marriage system, the caste or class system'. The films function as tools for eliciting attitudes and views on salient themes; family affairs and problems, romance, courtship, and marriage were often discussed. There is a recurrent recognition of the 'influence' and value of the films in the lives of girls in particular. There are frequent references to the 'meanings, the really deep meanings, which reflect the way we think, it's just so . . . so . . . so I don't know, so influential'.

It would appear that Hindi films can serve to legitimate a particular view of the world and at the same time to open up contradictions within it. So while young people sometimes use films to deconstruct 'traditional culture' many parents use them to foster certain 'traditional' attitudes, values and beliefs in their children. Films are expected to have both an entertainment and a didactic function and are seen by parents as useful agents of cultural continuity and as contributing to the (re)-formation of cultural identity.

Various degrees of scepticism are registered among the boys about parents' attempts to 'artifically maintain a culture' through film: 'Parents want their children to maintain certain religious values, beliefs and customs but that doesn't mean that Indian films are necessarily going to educate them in that way. They may well do the opposite . . . I think the moral standards in most recent films is pretty appalling.' But clear distinctions are made between religion and a sense of cultural identity and whilst firmly upholding the Sikh faith one boy claims: 'Parents use the films to represent their culture to their children but that will not work because those are not my roots, that place [India] has nothing to do with me anymore.'

Many parents lament what they see as a process of progressive 'cultural loss' in each generation of children. Looking to the past they attempt to re-create 'traditional culture'. Meanwhile young people, with eyes to the future, are busy re-creating something 'new'. The striving after cultural continuity and the negotiation of cultural identity are thus inescapably dialectical processes and they must, moreover, be seen in the widest possible context. The notion of viewing as a social activity which takes place in families needs to be extended to include more detailed explorations of the wider social, cultural, and ideological contexts and uses of the VCR.

What is clear is that for the young people interviewed a sense of ethnic, national, and cultural identity does not displace or dominate the equally lived and formed identities based on age, gender, peer group, and neighbourhood. Static notions of culture are extremely disabling as are absolutist views of black-and-white cultures as fixed, mutually impermeable expressions of 'racial' or national identity. Notions of national culture with unique customs and practices understood as 'pure' homogenous nationality need to be challenged.

One is reminded in this context of the arguments put forward by Benedict Anderson (1983) about the use of cultural artefacts in constructing 'imagined communities' based on notions of nation and nationness. The 'imagined communities', constructed and created through the viewing of films on VCR may link Asian communities across the world. However, these communities, with their origins in history and experience, are not fixed but change, develop and combine, and are in turn redispersed in historic processes.

If cultural practices are detached from their origins they can be used to found and extend new patterns of communication which can give rise to new common identities. Perhaps most of all this study provides a contemporary example of how 'traditional' ties are created and recreated out of present rather than past conditions.

Brunel University, London, England

Notes

1 This paper is based on a dissertation submitted for MA Film and Television Studies for Education, University of London Institute of Education, 1987.
2 The term 'Indian' film is used most commonly by interviewees but distinctions between films are also drawn according to language (i.e. Hindi, Panjabi, and Urdu) as well genre.
3 See, for example, Ballard (1979) and Community Relations Commission (1979), and for a critique of such perspectives see Parmar (1981).
4 This estimated figure is based on surveys carried out in three Southall schools.
5 Lutze (1985).
6 Gundara (1986).
7 Other contexts documented in the research included siblings viewing together in the home, viewing with friends/peers, women/girls-only groups, women solo viewing and male-only viewing.
8 For further accounts of family contexts of viewing see, for example, Morley (1986); Simpson (1987).
9 For a more detailed exploration of narration in the popular Hindi film see Thomas (1985).

References

Anderson, Benedict (1983) *Imagined Communities*. London: Verso.
Ballard, Catherine (1979) 'Conflict, continuity and change: second generation Asians', in V. Saifullah Khan (ed.) *Minority Families in Britain*. London: Macmillan.
Community Relations Commission (1979) *Between Two Cultures: A Study of the Relationship between Generations in the Asian Community*. London: Community Relations Commission.
Gundara, Jagdish (1986) 'Education in a multicultural society', in Gundara *et al.* (eds) *Racism, Diversity and Education*. London: Hodder & Stoughton.
Lutze (1985) 'From Bharata to Bombay: change and continuity in Hindi film aesthetics', in B. Pfleiderer (ed.) *The Hindi Film: Agent and Re-Agent of Cultural Change*. Manohar: 7.
Mishra, Vijay (1985) 'Towards a theoretical critique of Bombay Cinema', *Screen*, 26 (3–4).
Morley, David (1986) *Cultural Power and Domestic Leisure*. London: Comedia.
Palmer, Patricia (1986) *The Lively Audience*. London: Allen & Unwin.
Parmar, Pratibha (1981) 'Young Asian women: a critique of the pathological approach'. *Multi-Racial Education*, 10 (1).
Saarti, Anil (1985) in B. Pfleiderer (ed.) *The Hindi Film: Agent and Re-Agent of Cultural Change*. Manohar: 23.
Simpson, Philip (ed.) (1987) *Parents Talking*. London: Comedia.
Thomas, Rosie (1985) 'Indian cinema pleasures and popularity'. *Screen*, 26 (3–4): 123–35.

GABRIELE KREUTZNER

ON DOING CULTURAL STUDIES IN WEST GERMANY

Among the major items on my schedule for a research trip to the United States in 1986 were a number of appointments with scholars involved in the study of the role of the media in contemporary culture. On the occasion of one of these meetings, I was invited to participate in a small conference at the Department of Media Ecology, New York University. Somewhere in upstate New York's beautiful countryside, we listened to and discussed papers, ranging from the revolution in the doctor–patient relationship brought about by the invention of the stethoscope to the input of the computer into new ways of thinking and writing. Under the spell of the impressions that weekend had left me with, I followed the invitation to visit one of the department's courses for doctoral candidates the following week. I don't remember the book that was supposed to be analysed at that particular session. What I do remember very well, however, is the kind of discussion that emerged during that session. When initial questions concerning critical evaluations didn't produce too much of an enthusiastic response in class, the three professors started to comment upon that work from their differing perspectives, and soon an extremely lively controversy emerged involving almost everyone present and covering an amazing range of issues and problems. Walking home two hours later, my mind still in the midst of the discussion, it occurred to me how much these past two hours had helped me to clarify my own position. And for the first time in a long time, I had experienced an academic controversy not only as inspiring, but also as extremely pleasurable.

Of course, my reconstruction of this experience omits any analytical account of the conditions under which such academic and intellectual controversy is likely to emerge, nor does it touch upon issues of politics and power that are inextricably related to any academic/intellectual dispute. But what this incident signifies for me is the insight into the necessity of a *Streitkultur* (a culture of controversy) informed by the widest possible range of differing voices which I have come to see as a prerequisite for the development of critical thinking about culture and society. And while a *Streitkultur* does not necessarily manifest itself as the kind of cosy and harmonious enterprise evoked by my little anecdote, I think that such a context is essential for the emergence of a productive as well as pleasurable critical discourse.

It is such a *Streitkultur* about cultural phenomena that I miss in West German academic and intellectual life. And while the 'discovery' of a variety of recent critical work on contemporary culture done in Australia, Great Britain, and the United States has contributed in no small way to my political motivation and my pleasure in cultural studies, in West Germany there does not seem to be any widely shared conviction that to study contemporary culture in its heterogeneity and diversity is politically and theoretically significant and that critical thinking can and should be something plea-surable.

This is not to say, however, that there is no such thing as cultural studies in this country. Indeed, one can trace a range of spaces in West German academic and intellectual life today where cultural studies (in the sense of the approach developed by the British Centre for Contemporary Cultural Studies) have emerged. As in Great Britain, the 1970s saw the development of the history workshop movement; lately, *Alltagsgeschichte* (everyday life history) has made its contributions to the field. Furthermore, the Argument Verlag in West Berlin provides an outlet for projects which can be subsumed under the label of cultural studies. As its editorial committee puts it, the publishing house is dedicated to 'a theoretical culture of the Left'. Of particular interest to me are various projects that developed around the 'critical psychology' group. For example, a number of feminist projects studying everyday life history in terms of the constitution of the gendered subject has been published since 1980 (Haug, 1984; Haug and Hauser, 1985, 1986). These publications present the collective practices by women in Hamburg and West Berlin of writing and analysing their own autobio-graphical accounts, and thereby seeking to understand and change their positions within patriarchal ideology. Recently, the 'critical psychology' group has done research on *Ausländerfeindlichkeit*, investigating specific forms of xenophobia and racism in West Germany. While this work is yet to be published, a project of this type is of particular importance in the context context of the current tightening of the terms under which western European countries are prepared to offer political asylum to refugees from countries such as the Lebanon, Iran and Chile. The 'critical psychology' group not only analyses the broad functions of racism in the current climate of economic recession and political (neo-)conservatism, but also in a more concrete sense is concerned with the specifically bureaucratic forms of racism experienced by these refugees.

In a more restricted sense, the work of the Ludwig-Uhland-Institut für empirische Kulturwissenschaft (LUI) in Tübingen has to be seen as the outstanding example of cultural studies in a firmly institutionalized academic context. Based on a concept of culture as something which is alive and lived, the work done in Tübingen's tiny institute stresses the historical determinacy of cultural processes. The projects carried out in the past decade include some of the rare examples of women's studies in West Germany.[1] As to the historical specificities of German culture, a LUI project has recently finished a study of everyday life under Nazism in the Tübingen vicinity (LUI, 1988). Doing field work in various villages, the group interviewed inhabitants about their lives between 1933 and 1945. As part of their work, they published weekly articles in the local newspaper for several months about different aspects of everyday life under Nazism. Such a study clearly rejects the notion that German Fascism can be seen as something which was injected into the population in 1933 by Nazi propaganda, while re-education or *die Gnade der späten Geburt* ('the mercy of being born during or after the War', as chancellor Kohl has put it) provided the remedy by which Nazi ideology was 'neutralized'. Moreover, it helps us to understand how Fascism 'worked' in concrete everyday life practices – something which abstract theories of Fascism (important as they are) cannot provide.

Another area of research at the LUI in the 1980s was the study of the role of the mass media in the lives of their audiences. For a number of years, Hermann Bausinger, Klaus Jensen, and Jan-Uwe Rogge have investigated the media in the context of everyday life in the family (but also in other forms of personal existence). Bausinger, Jensen, and Rogge did not restrict their study to any particular medium, but sought to investigate the significance of the technological environment as a whole (from newspaper to radio, to television, the VCR, and the computer) in domestic life. While presently media research is not a prominent part of the work done at the LUI, the range and the kinds of studies carried out at the institute represent the finest examples of cultural studies in the West German academic system.

As my brief and rather eclectic account suggests, something like cultural studies is alive in West Germany, if not exactly kicking. But whereas projects and initiatives such as those pointed out above are significant contributions to the international discussion about culture, the field as a whole remains underdeveloped in West Germany. The problems confronting the development of cultural studies in West Germany today range from the lack of academic institutionalization, the severe monetary restrictions imposed upon the academic/educational system during the past years to the 'no future' perspective in terms of academic positions. But while such limitations and problems have an international dimension, there is also a specific difficulty that cultural studies face in this country, in so far as the range of discussion about (contemporary) culture and its political functions and social determinations remains very limited. And although there are signs that interactions between various approaches and disciplines emerge on a local level, a peculiar kind of indifference to problems of contemporary culture – especially in the humanities – prevents the development of innovative thinking. As someone with a background in literature and language, it is particularly the humanities' indifference that fuels a good deal of discontent on my part. Moreover, I see this uninterest as the disciplines' active contribution to their gradual degeneration into a position of sociocultural insignificance – a sort of intellectual version of collective hara-kiri. I am not going to provide a thorough analysis of the humanities' current predicament in West Germany. Instead, I want to indicate some of the major problems in the attempt to study culture in West Germany.

(1) In West Germany, there is no parallel to the work of scholarly intellectuals such as Raymond Williams. If the 'New Left' in Great Britain challenged dominant concepts of culture in the Arnoldian vein, this also resulted in changes in terms of what was taught at British universities and polytechnics (Bromley and Oakley, 1986). Furthermore, such challenges brought about a considerable expansion of the humanities' traditional concerns. I am prepared to accept notes of protest should I construct a myth here, but to my knowledge the Centre for Contemporary Cultural Studies itself grew out of a graduate course in English. Similarly, those fields which have made major contributions to cultural studies in the US – such as film and television studies, feminist studies, etc. – often sprang from the literature departments. While there have been (and still are) various attempts to open up the traditional language and literature departments in West Germany, e.g. to include the study of film, the investigation of these new 'territories' are carried out under the firm dominance of traditional literary criticism and its underlying premises.

(2) While the 1960s saw the critical reception of Marxist approaches in the humanities (such as the work of Adorno, Benjamin, Horkheimer, Lukács), the 1970s brought a freeze in terms of political and theoretical debates. In the 1960s and early 1970s, the *Germanistik* departments went through a lively phase of intellectual dispute. Simultaneously, the academic agenda expanded to include the study of 'mass literature', television series, etc. While courses offering the study of cultural texts excluded from the 'proper' literary canon continued throughout the 1970s, there was and is little (if any) attention paid to the Marxist paradigms which became so influential in British and US cultural analyses. My first encounter with theorists such as Althusser and Gramsci was through my discovery of *Screen*, not through a film course or through academic training.[2] Today, the interpretation of culture in a Marxist tradition is generally restricted to the application of the 'classical approaches' to culture – i.e. to Critical Theory and economic determinism (Grossberg, 1984). While this country saw the emergence of a strong women's movement (up to the mid-1970s), it did not have the same kind of impact on the academic world that it did in Great Britain and the US. If it was particularly in areas such as film and television studies that feminism developed its vanguard position, there was (and still is) no such distinguished 'field' as film and television studies in the West German academic system.[3] Moreover, academic jobs have rarely been available to women and, in spite of various affirmative action efforts, the situation has not considerably improved in the 1980s. Furthermore, there is little evidence of a critical reception of post-structuralist and postmodernist approaches (Gulliver, 1986: 55–7). The adjective 'critical' is important

here: I do not suggest that this country's academic and intellectual scene should simply adopt the various British and US approaches to culture that became so important in my own thinking. But I do suggest that an active encounter with these international trends in cultural studies could overcome the current stagnation of critical thought in West Germany.

(3) The severe cuts in terms of budgets and staff within the universities and the educational system that came along with the conservative *Wende* (the turning point) from the 1970s to the 1980s have affected the humanities – and particularly the literature and language departments – much more drastically than the natural sciences or the field of engineering (Krugmann, 1986: 12). Also, the chances of those who enter the job market with a university education in the humanities are – to put it euphemistically – quite unpromising. All in all, the developments of the past decade have arguably led to a 'legitimation crisis' of the humanities (Gulliver, 1986: 5).

Lately, cultural neo-conservatives have come to the field's rescue by introducing the so-called 'compensation theory' into the changed political climate of the 1980s.[4] Essentially, this 'theory' is based on the following argument: with the increased modernization of the contemporary world, the humanities become indispensable; they are essential to modern society. So far so good – the trouble occurs when one asks why the humanities are seen as essential and what functions are ascribed to them. If the humanities can be described as an ensemble of disciplines and fields of inquiry engaged in the study of culture, the crucial point is the concept of culture activated by compensation theorists. It is a concept which takes up what Herman Bausinger has described as culturally specific notions of *Kultur* which – writing in 1980 – he rightly hesitated to dismiss as belonging to the past (Bausinger, 1980). Based on the opposition between *Zivilisation* and *Kultur*, technological and social development is written into the sphere of *Zivilisation*, while *Kultur* is constructed ahistorically, as the incarnation of tradition – in short, as the (great) cultural heritage. While compensation theorists accept technological change and social modernization as inevitable (while some regrets may be expressed), they reject cultural change and cultural modernization. *Kultur*, then, is always a thing of the past which has to be preserved and mediated. *Kultur* provides the individual with a sense of identity and endowes contemporary life with meaning.

As to the compensation theorists' definition of the humanities as 'affirmative' sciences, little protest (if any) has been expressed from within the field. Meanwhile, the 'theory' has been adopted as a handy platform for neo-conservative cultural politics (Schnädelbach, 1988: 35). There seems to be little willingness or ability on the academic community's part to challenge this neoconservative discourse, and I do not expect that such challenges would all speak the same political language.

Writing in 1979, Winfried Fluck noted that the loss of social prestige which the humanities had to face through the advance of the natural sciences and of positivism was experienced by the literary intelligentsia in terms of an overall cultural decay (7). While the officially acknowledged demand for individuals trained in language and literature (as future teachers in the

Gymnasien) granted these disciplines an unchallenged status in the 1960s and early 1970s, recent developments have caught them quite unprepared (Krugmann, 1986: 13). If the literary intelligentsia's relation to the social has traditionally been informed by notions of cultural doom and decay throughout the century, the recent 'crisis' has reinforced this gloomy perspective.

(4) Finally, what troubles me most is that left discourses about popular culture are still dominated by the economistic and idealist assumptions of Frankfurt School Critical Theory. I refer particularly to the German Left's very abstract notion of the colonization of consciousness by the culture industries. But what are the reasons for the West German intelligentsia's preference for such assumptions? Why are the theoretical developments which shape much of the current thinking in Great Britain and the US (as the nationally specific critical contexts that I am familiar with) practically ignored in West Germany? For one thing, one has to consider the historically specific conditions of West German intellectual culture which was virtually destroyed by Nazism. Even now, Germany suffers from the exodus forced upon most of its finest intellectuals and artists of that time. And although many of them came back after 1945, Left intellectual culture could not just simply be taken up from where it had ceased to exist in 1933. I suspect that as a result of German history, intellectuals on the left have taken on the heritage of an overdetermined hostility toward 'popular' phenomena. This is not to say that anything 'popular' is automatically rejected by those on the Left. Thus, it is a common practice in the (Left) 'alternative' cultural scenes to supply their public events with music from South America, from Greece, Turkey, etc. But such celebration of traditional music not only signifies a (romantic) desire for an 'authentic' popular culture. It also suggests that the search for popular phenomena with which they can identify leads the German intellectual outside of her or his immediate cultural context. In contrast to this, cultural phenomena popular with broad strata of the people – and especially with the German people – are dismissed as ideology pure and simple. In Britain and the United States writers such as Williamson (1986) and Modleski (1987) have recently criticized those who can be seen as merely celebrating popular culture. However, academic and intellectual discourses in West Germany have yet to open up for the theoretical possibility of contradiction and conflict between processes of cultural production and consumption. In this respect, it is the Frankfurt School positions, and particularly their reception by the 1968 movement, which stand against such an opening up of 'Left' discourses on culture in this country. A good deal of writing has covered the specificities of the German 1968 movement as a rebellion of those born immediately after the war against their fathers (and the gender identification is intentional here). It was this male dominance in the movement which was later challenged by female activists, a historical point which can be seen as the beginning of the women's movement in West Germany. However, the conventional construct of 1968 as a generational (and gender-specific)– conflict in postwar Germany (i.e. as the sons' rebellion against their 'bad' fathers) overlooks for

one thing that the 1968 movement also chose a number of 'good' fathers. Among the chosen ones were the Frankfurt School critics. I don't have to elaborate on the significance of figures such as Adorno, Horkheimer, and Marcuse (among others) for the West German 1968 movement. Instead, let me point to a specific correspondence between the Frankfurters and the 1968 movement which I see as lying in the parallel between the former's powerful attack on the culture industries and the latter's interpretation of their immediate experiences. The movement's continuous denouncement in the media, especially in the Springer press, caused numerous demonstrations in front of Springer buildings. Even more importantly, the mass media in general, and Springer in particular, were held responsible for the fact that the 'masses' did not join the students in the streets. Here, the Frankfurt School's attack on the culture industries suggested itself as a rationale for the frustrating state of affairs: blinded by ideology (imposed upon them by the media), the 'masses' acted against their own interests by staying at home (in front of their television sets). If the movement's avant-garde was right in pointing to the political power held by Springer and others, it did not analyse the historical origins of Adorno/Horkheimer's determinist perspective. After all, their theory served as a convenient 'explanation' why revolution did not come about.

The university reforms of the early 1970s helped many of those politicized around 1968 to acquire leading positions in the academic system, and the job market situation at that time allowed this academic generation to acquire important positions in the media, the educational system, and other important areas of social life. It is significant to note the disjunction between what happened (and did not happen) inside and outside of academic and intellectual culture in this period. Oppositional *politics* in the 1970s began to involve groups who differed from the 1968 movement (which was dominated by male, middle-class, and traditional Left groups). This expansion of Left political practices was not restricted to the categories of gender and generation, but also implied the involvement of groups such as unemployed urban youth and, although less visibly, ethnic communities. But whereas oppositional political practices were reproduced through historical modifications, Left *theoretical* practices essentially remained under the dominance of a critical tradition preserving its determinist assumptions toward the cultural. These assumptions have become part of the Left intellectual *habitus* (Bourdieu, 1979), an ingredient of the complex set of fixed dispositions by which this cultural group is socially reproduced.

Within this Left intellectual *habitus* the overall cultural situation is persistently reconstructed as being over-determined by the all-pervasive power of the culture industry. In this construct, the politically progressive subject is positioned *outside* of the culture industries' ideological practices. However, in defence of the culture industry's all-pervasive power, the progressive subject is granted the capacity of seeing right through the manipulations of popular/mass culture that affect 'other' social and subcultural groups so fatally. Ascribing total power to the culture industries and perceiving of those who consume mass culture as forever lost to dominant ideology, it is only logical – and also an unequivocal sign of a politically 'progressive' attitude – that Left intellectuals then sneer at mass culture and prefer not to deal with it seriously at all.

This 'preferred attitude' is linked to another widely held assumption, namely that culture (naturally) can be divided into 'good' and 'bad' objects. In Left perspectives, the point of departure can be seen in the Frankfurt School's distinction between (good) high culture (i.e. selected works of modernism) and (bad) mass culture. Of course, since the time of Adorno and Horkheimer the good/bad dichotomy has been modified and made more complex, but without throwing into doubt the absolute, abstract, and universal characteristics of such categorizations and value judgements. Today, one dividing line is usually drawn between film as art, as auteur cinema, as the non-commercial 'great works' versus film as mass entertainment à la Hollywood. While the former tends to be celebrated, the latter is unequivocally condemned (and mostly rejected as an inadequate object of serious investigation). The ultimate line, however, is drawn when it comes to television.[5] Recently, the metaphor of the 'flood of images' has quite frequently popped up in discourses on the medium's impact on contemporary society and culture. Two years ago, the conservative attempts to find support for their repressive policies towards political refugees were articulated through the image of the *Asylantenflut* (the flood of those seeking sanctuary in West Germany). While this metaphor was widely criticized on the left by pointing to its Fascist tradition – well-known through Klaus Theweleit's analysis of the 'red flood' metaphor (1980) – the same imagery is unproblematically taken up in discourses on television. What unites these otherwise quite different uses of the 'flood' metaphor are the notions of danger and of an absolute threat called up by the invocation of something without shape and form, something transgressing all boundaries, something beyond control. In the present situation, while commercial television is gradually being established in West Germany, the Left intelligentsia articulates its concerns with television through the image of it as an uncontrollable threat to the individual. The only way to escape – so it seems – is by turning away from it.

To avoid misunderstandings: I think that the Left (regardless of cultural and national specificities) has an obligation to continue the investigation and critique of the culture industries' economic and political power. This is all the more important in a situation in which the industries have 'learned' to address their audiences as consumers. But if there is a 'critical' potential implied in our historically determined ambivalences toward the cultural, it is not constructively used to advance critical thinking in West Germany. Instead, the discourses on mass/popular culture remain informed by the belief in universal and absolute notions of cultural and aesthetic value and by an unreflected contempt for mass culture (*and* its consumers). While intellectuals in West Germany can take as their point of departure the Frankfurt School's insistence on a 'critical' theory of society and on the analysis of heterogeneous forms of domination, it is certainly high time to leave the paternal house of Critical Theory (Hansen, 1987: 39). If the history of this country gives Germans the responsibility to be especially sensitive to questions of power and domination, such a sensibility could enrich international debate about contemporary culture in which – as Stuart Hall has recently pointed out – there is the danger that questions of hegemony and power become suppressed (Hall, 1988). In the light of the radical cultural changes that lie ahead of us, it will be politically disastrous if the Left in West Germany continues to ignore the heterogeneity of cultural life – and particularly the terrain of popular culture – as an area in which political struggles are fought out.

Universität Tübingen, West Germany

Notes

1 Let me point to Carola Lipp's historical work and to the feminist ethnographic work carried out by Jutta Dornheim, Susanne Sackstetter and others.
2 It should be noted, however, that Joachim Paech *et al.* (University of Osnabrück) have edited a book on *Screen* theory during a short period in which film studies were offered in Osnabrück: *Screen Theory: Zehn Jahre Filmtheorie in England von 1971 bis 1981*. Osnabrück, 1985.
3 If *Frauen und Film* is a relevant contribution to the wider debate about film culture, it is significant to note that this publication sprang directly from the women's movement (as well as from women's involvement in film practices) and that most of the women in the editorial collective do not hold academic positions.
4 More detailed discussions of the 'compensation theory' are provided in *Kursbuch 91: Wozu Geisteswissenschaften?* Berlin: Kursbuch Verlag, 1988.
5 Charlotte Brunsdon (forthcoming) discusses discourses on television in her essay on 'Gender and Genre', in *Remote Control: Television Audiences and Cultural Power*, edited by Ellen Seiter, Hans Borchers, Gabriele Kreutzner and Eva-Maria Warth. London and New York: Routledge.

References

Bausinger, Hermann (1980) 'Zur Problematik des Kulturbegriffs', in A. Wierlacher (ed.) *Fremdsprache Deutsch. Grundlagen und Verfahren der Fremdsprachenphilologie*. Bd. 1. München: Wilhelm Fink: 57–69.
Bourdieu, Pierre (1979/1972) *Entwurf einer Theorie der Praxis*. (Orig.: *Esquisse d'une Théorie de la Pratique, précédé de trois études d'etnologie kabyle*) Trans. Cordula Pialoux and Bernd Schwibs. Frankfurt: Suhrkamp.
Bromley, Roger and Oakley, John (1986) 'Cultural studies in Britain today', in B. P. Lange and R. Lehberger (eds) *Gulliver. Anglistik Heute. Einsichten und Aussichten*. Berlin: Argument: 113–22.
Fluck, Winfried (1979) *Populäre Kultur. Ein Studienbuch zur Funktionsbestimmung und Interpretation populärer Kultur*. Stuttgart: Metzler.
Grossberg, Lawrence (1984) 'Strategies of Marxist cultural interpretation'. *Critical Studies in Mass Communications*, 1 (4): 392–421.
Gulliver (1986) 'Probleme, Perspektiven, Prioritäten einer kritischen Anglistik. Ein Rundgespräch'. *Gulliver. Anglistik Heute*: 57–77.

Hall, Stuart (1988) 'The changing patterns of television in the nineties'. Opening Address to the Third International Television Studies Conference, London.

Hansen, Miriam (1987) 'Messages in a bottle? (Miriam Hansen Examines 'Frauen und Film', Women's Cinema and Feminist Film Theory in West Germany)'. *Screen*, 28 (4): 30–9.

Haug, Frigga (ed.) (1983) *Frauenformen 2. Sexualisierung*. Berlin: Argument.

—— (1984) *Frauenformen. Alltagsgeschichten und Entwurf einer Theorie weiblicher Sozialisation*. Berlin: Argument.

Haug, F. and Hauser, K. (eds) (1985) *Subjekt Frau. Kritische Psychologie der Frauen*. Bd. 1. Berlin: Argument.

—— (1986) *Der Widerspenstigen Lähmung. Kritische Psychologie der Frauen*. Bd. 2. Berlin: Argument.

Kursbuch 91 (1988) *Wozu Geisteswissenschaften?*

Krugmann, Malte C. (1986) 'Anglistik nach den Reformen. *Gulliver*. 20: 12–56.

Lipp, Carola (1986) 'Ledige Mütter, "Huren" und "Lumpenhunde." Sexualmoral und Ehrenhändel im Arbeitermilieu des 19. Jahrhunderts', in U. Jeggle *et al.* (eds) *Tübinger Beiträge zur Volkskultur*. Tübingen: Tübinger Vereinigung für Volkskunde E.V.

Ludwig-Uhland-Institut für empirische Kulturwissenschaft der Universität Tübingen (1988) *Nationalsozialismus im Landkreis Tübingen. Eine Heimatkunde*. Tübingen: Tübinger Chronik.

Modleski, Tania (1987) 'Introduction', in her (ed.) *Studies in Entertainment. Critical Approaches to Mass Culture*. Bloomington and Indianapolis: Indiana University Press, 1987: ix–xix.

Schnädelbach, Helmut (1988) 'Kritik der Kompensationstheorie'. *Kursbuch*, 91: 35–46.

Theweleit, Klaus (1980) *Männerphantasien. 1. Frauen, Fluten, Körper, Geschichte*. Reinbek bei Hamburg: Rowohlt.

Williamson, Judith (1986) 'The problems of being popular'. *New Socialist*, September: 14–15.

BILL SCHWARZ

POPULAR CULTURE: THE LONG MARCH

■ Susan Easton, Alun Howkins, Stuart Laing, Lind Merricks and Helen Walker, *Disorder and Discipline. Popular culture from 1550 to the present* (Aldershot, Temple Smith, 1988), 215 pp., £18.50.

Some of the individual authors of *Disorder and Discipline* have demonstrated in other quarters admirable intellectual skills – Alun Howkins' *Poor Labouring Men*, for example, or Stuart Laing's *Representations of Working-Class Life*.[1] For a decade or more all the authors have sustained an innovative, creative course; and in this day and age to produce in addition a book arising from collective teaching is indeed to battle against the odds, as many of us have experienced with considerably less to show for it. But the volume which has emerged is pretty ropey. The current overproduction in publishing depends upon indiscriminate appropriation: a contract is hustled into being in conjunction with a few suitably modish bottles of Frascati, a book stitched together which skims the boom until it dips from sight, the new list submerging the old.

Two short early chapters chart the development of popular culture from 1550 to 1914 – a breathtaking task, reminiscent of a collection from the same locale, the Yeos' *Popular Culture and Class Conflict, 1590–1914*. These initial chapters provide necessarily abbreviated, descriptive accounts, asserting the case for the chosen periodization (they divide the epoch at 1700) rather than demonstrating or arguing their case. Rich, sophisticated analyses of popular culture, of which Underdown's *Revel, Riot and Rebellion* provides a case in point, get squashed and pummelled into servicing an abstract, generalized, sub-Bakhtinian notion of carnival.[2]

Three further short chapters deal historically with the twentieth century, focusing on leisure in the interwar period, the development of the mass media from 1900–50, and the role of television. The links between the chapters remain uninvestigated. The implicit assumption about the centrality of the mass media in the reorganization of modern popular cultures, surely correct, remains only implicit. The use of source material is intriguingly selective. I find it surprising for example that no reference at all is made to the work of Scannell and Cardiff on the history of the BBC and broadcasting.[3] The chapter on television is devoted as much to a speedy run-through of the various methodological approaches as it is to television itself, making the chapter sit oddly in the collection as a whole.

A final chapter is devoted to gender, a concept not notably prominent in the preceding pages. The object taken here is the sexual differentiation of youth subcultures, looking to masculine soccer cultures and, amongst girls and young women, the role of romance. Much of this derives from work done at the Centre for Contemporary Cultural Studies in Birmingham in the 1970s, especially a series of papers produced then, and subsequently, by Angela McRobbie.[4]

The book is, literally, inconclusive, so any more general hints about the thematic and conceptual organization of the collection must derive from the preface and introduction. The preface provides an interesting resumé of the course from which the book draws, Popular Culture, Leisure and the Social Order, founded at the University of Sussex in 1975. As the authors suggest, the influence of 1970s social history functioned as the primary intellectual paradigm, and this explains the preoccupation with leisure and with the idea of social control, a concept closely associated at the time with the study of popular pastimes. The methodological difficulties attendant upon notions of social control are recognized, in particular with reference to a distinguished essay by Gareth Stedman Jones from the same period, although my feeling is that this recognition is nonetheless laced with some reluctance to let go of the basic problematic. These overriding concerns unsettle the authors' claim that the volume in hand 'examines historical changes in popular culture from the standpoint of current theoretical debates' (p. viii), for their conceptual purview is both dated and narrow. It is ironic that they should begin with Stuart Hall's 'Notes on deconstructing the "popular"', a paper delivered to the mind-bending, schismatic History Workshop Conference of 1979, for nowhere in the collection is the deconstructive twist in Hall's argument ever taken up.[5] In fact the vision of popular culture which emerges from these pages looks depressingly uniform, from epoch to epoch, poised in some suspended resistance to an undeclared, unspecified antagonist. In this context their discussion of Richard Hoggart, Denys Thompson, and Christopher Bigsby is not out of order, but nor is it particularly gripping.

The authors also use the introduction to undertake a synoptic account of the development of what we now take to be cultural studies and the study of popular culture. The familiar terrain is surveyed, from Hoggart onwards, taking in the see-saw of culturalism and structuralism, and through on to the impact of feminism. They give a welcome, though for me confused and confusing, emphasis to the contribution of historiography to the overall emergence of cultural studies, and in so doing they raise the important issue of periodization. This appears inevitably as a central problem in a book of this type – significantly it was exactly with this that Stuart Hall began his 'Notes on deconstructing the "popular"' – although the only resolution adopted in this volume is the practical division between the chapters, with too little explanation of the overarching historical schema. It is, or should be, precisely a theoretical issue. I'll return to this in a moment.

If there is some ambiguity about the historical issues, one point is made trenchantly, and it conforms to the substantive readings of popular forms in the chapters which follow. This is the supposition that the study of popular culture in itself is 'a scandal in the eyes of established academic disciplines' (p. 2), 'a scandal to the seriousness (*sic*) of much of the formal institution of education' (p. 23). It is, according to the authors, frequently condemned for its 'treasonable and transgressive character' (p. 5). They even make the inventive suggestion that 'By the early Seventies Cultural Studies had both outgrown and become rather ashamed of its humble origins in the study of popular culture'; indeed 'there remains a sense in which the attempt to consign some of the original concerns of *The Uses of Literacy* (and of the first years of the Birmingham Research Centre) to the sphere of the insignificant was merely to reproduce the knee-jerk reflexes of the established academy. It is perhaps understandable that as Cultural Studies attained its "legal majority" and as it attempted to overwhelm existing disciplines by the weight of its theoretical sophistication and the seriousness of its scholarship it should attempt to cover the traces of its illegitimate origins . . .' (p. 15). Much of the evidence for this comes from an old essay by Colin Sparks published in a long-forgotten issue of *Working Papers in Cultural Studies*.[6] Sparks himself occupies a singular position within the field of cultural studies, as he would be the first to declare. But even then, his argument – strident and time-worn as its tone now appears – is basically no more than a polemical appeal for students of cultural studies to put an end to uncritical nostalgia for the past culture of a subordinate class, a view which today would find few dissidents. Their more pointed proposition that cultural studies at some moment disowned its concern with the popular is not, in my experience, one which makes much sense. Nor am I convinced that the study of popular culture within the formal education system is as intrinsically subversive as the authors of this volume would wish.

Two general comments come to mind, the first to do with race, the second returning to the question of periodization. Race, or ethnic identity, hardly touches the pages of *Disorder and Discipline*. To say this, of course, can smack as empty posturing for arguably the fault runs less through this or that particular book than through the intellectual organization of the field as a whole. No doubt the authors themselves would willingly admit the need for work on race to be deepened and extended, so there is nothing in contention here. Still, it's worth recording the fact that a book which takes us from sixteenth-century England to the present makes no mention of empire and all its cultural ramifications. But the point which strikes me is this. There exist now any number of articles which tell the story of the formation of cultural studies, an untroubled memory spontaneously summoning the figures of Hoggart, Williams, and Thompson. In some respects the development of cultural studies has for long carried a peculiarly English identity, the nationality of the discipline's foremost practitioner, Raymond Williams, notwithstanding. A subsequent obsession generated within the field for the totem of Englishness often can seem to link it forever with an unspoken insularity, the critiques mobius-like, turning in on themselves. Perhaps the legacy of the Lewises has been more enduring than many of us would care to admit. But there is also a measure of amnesia here. The earliest moments of cultural studies – the late 1950s and the early 1960s – exactly coincided with, and were in part determined by, the final moments in the disintegration of empire. This period, too, represents a critical moment in the historic rendezvous of a black population – the imperial citizenry of a previous imagination – with the metropolitan nation. 'Race', dramatically and violently, reordered perceptions of the domestic polity. *Uses of Literacy, The Long Revolution, The Making of the English Working Class* – these may be ranked as formative texts. But so too were other voices formative in this period. Lessing tells her story of empire; C. L. R. James in *Beyond a Boundary* provides an indication of what the 'culture and society' traditions and the practices of Englishness could look like 'from underneath'.[7] Hall and Whannel, and Francis Newton (aka E. J. Hobsbawm) reconstruct the roots of rhythm and blues, *the* great resource of a burgeoning white youth culture.[8] Early editions of *New Left Review*, it is instructive if dispiriting to recall, carried notices urging support for the ANC and for an economic boycott against apartheid. This was the time not only of Suez, but of Sharpeville, the Congo, Algeria – and white riots in West London. It was these concerns which, in part, provided an imperative to investigate the culture of the imperial nation. And, moreover, like many such previous groups of 'English' intellectuals, this was overwhelmingly an *emigré* intelligentsia: in the influential Oxford Socialist Club of the mid- and late 1950s, which put together *The Universities and Left Review*, 'there was . . . a moment when the Welsh, Scots and colonials took a look around the room and came to the startling conclusion that "There is not an Englishman among us"'.[9] In short, my guess is that this *emigré* status brought with it a significant, attendant preoccupation with race and empire in what we might call early cultural studies, and that this preoccupation subsequently dipped from view and has only recently been recovered. But whatever the case it sounds increasingly implausible to go on telling the story of the formation of cultural studies without paying due heed to these dimensions; and it highlights too the weakened explanatory value of a cultural analysis which ignores race and ethnicity.

The second comment touches upon questions raised – on occasion bafflingly and preposterously – by the debates on postmodernism, and hence returns us to the problem of periodization. However arcane and infuriating these discussions can be, they are clearly on to *something*. And the likelihood is that we are coming to a time when the model which describes popular culture in a relation of antagonism to a high or elite culture is, in some senses, ceasing to be serviceable. The reason for this has precisely to do with the dynamics of popular culture as a capitalist culture.[10] For the great commodification of popular culture which coincided with what is variously described as mass society, monopoly capitalism, or the modernist epoch has had the effect, in subsequent decades, of eroding high culture as a determining field of force, just as the pessimists of the 1930s had feared. This is not to say that high culture has disappeared. It is merely to note that it no longer is able to exert the same force throughout the social formation, its authenticity no longer able to secure universal respect, its place taken – across classes – by mainstream pop music, TV soaps, the blockbuster movie, and so on. Capital accumulation has never exhibited much respect for traditions inherited from previous formations, and this applies to traditional intellectuals as much as to anything else. Since the thirties the theoreticians and upholders of high culture have been vocal in expressing their fear that they are about to be devoured. Not only does all 'melt into air', but from the same text we are reminded that 'The bourgeoisie has stripped of its halo every occupation hitherto honoured and looked to with reverent awe. It has converted the physician, the lawyer, the priest, the poet, the man of science, into its paid wage labourers'.[11] And, in the view of figures in the stamp of Walter Benjamin – never one much for halos and reverence – a good thing too. But if this is happening, if the old institutions of high culture are weakening, what then do we make of popular culture?

North-East London Polytechnic, England

Notes

1 Alun Howkins, *Poor Labouring Men. Rural radicalism in Norfolk, 1870–1923*, London, Routledge & Kegan Paul, 1985; Stuart Laing, *Representations of Working-Class Life, 1957–64*, London, Macmillan, 1986.

2 E. and S. Yeo (eds) *Popular Culture and Class Conflict, 1590–1914*, Brighton, Harvester, 1981; David Underdown, *Revel, Riot and Rebellion. Popular Politics and Culture in England, 1603–60*, Oxford, Clarendon, 1985.

3 See here, *inter alia*, their numerous contributions over the past decade to the journal *Media, Culture and Society*, London, Sage.

4 See, for example, Angela McRobbie's contributions to S. Hall and T. Jefferson (eds), *Resistance Through Rituals*, London, Hutchinson, 1976; Women's Studies Group (ed.), *Women Take Issue*, London, Hutchinson, 1978; and to A. McRobbie and M. Nava (eds), *Gender and Generation*, London, Macmillan, 1987; and Angela McRobbie, 'Settling accounts with subcultures', *Screen Education*, 34, 1980.

5 Stuart Hall, 'Notes on deconstructing the "popular"', in R. Samuel (ed.), *People's History and Socialist Theory*, London, Routledge & Kegan Paul, 1981; and Gareth Stedman Jones, 'Class expression *versus* social control?' *History Workshop Journal*, 4, 1977.

6 Colin Sparks, 'The abuses of literacy', *Working Papers in Cultural Studies*, 6, 1974; and for further reflections on this theme, 'The evolution of cultural studies', *Screen Education*, 22, 1977.

7 Many of Doris Lessing's novels carry this imprint, though it is most intense in the slightly later *The Four-Gated City*, first published 1969; C. L. R. James, *Beyond a Boundary*, London, Stanley Paul, 1963.

8 S. Hall and P. Whannel, *The Popular Arts*, London, Hutchinson, 1964; Francis Newton, *The Jazz Scene*, Harmondsworth, Penguin, 1961.

9 Stuart Hall, 'The Williams interviews' *Screen Education*, 34, 1980, p. 96; and see too Peter Worsley, 'Imperial retreat' in E. P. Thompson (ed.), *Out of Apathy*, London, Stevens, 1960.

10 For provocative reflections, Simon Frith, *Music For Pleasure*, Cambridge, Polity Press, 1988. He suggests: 'The rock era – born around 1956 with Elvis Presley, peaking around 1967 with *Sgt Pepper*, dying around 1976 with the Sex Pistols – turned out to be a by-way in the development of twentieth century popular music, rather than, as we thought at the time, any kind of mass cultural revolution. Rock was a last romantic attempt to preserve ways of music-making – performer as artist, performance as community – that had been made obsolete by technology and capital' (p. 1). However, a different view may appear if we think in terms of a plurality of distinct popular cultures, especially, in this instance, those organized around black cultures. See, *inter alia*, Paul Gilroy, *There Ain't No Black in the Union Jack*, London, Hutchinson, 1987; Dick Hebdige, *Cut 'N' Mix. Culture, Identity and Caribbean music*, London, Comedia/Methuen, 1987; Simon Jones, *Black Culture, White Youth. The Reggae Tradition from JA to UK*, London, Macmillan, 1988; and Les Back, 'Coughing up fire; soundsystems in south-east London.' *New Formations*, 5, 1988.

11 K. Marx and F. Engels, 'The Communist Manifesto', in K. Marx, *The Revolutions of 1848*, Harmondsworth, Penguin, 1973, p. 70.

LEN PALMER

SOME DOMINANT MYTHS OF OZ

■ J. Fiske, B. Hodge and G. Turner, *Myths of Oz: Reading Australian Popular Culture* (Sydney, Allen & Unwin, 1987), 191 pp.

T his is an interesting and accessible book. Through a semiotic analysis which views all cultural forms and practices as texts, the authors examine pubs and drinking, suburban homes and gardens, beaches, unemployment, shopping, tourism, public monuments, and the famous Australian accent. As a migrant Australian I found many new insights into aspects of Australian life.

Citing Barthes for their conception of myth the authors signal certain themes that can be used to make sense of Australian myths, for example the oppositions between culture/nature and public/private, even if the specific forms have parallels in other western countries. The selection covers 'high' cultural forms as well as 'popular' culture.

Of particular note is the attempt to relate much of their analysis of class, gender and certain aspects of ethnicity, specifically in relation to Aboriginal people. Class, gender, and ethnicity are not theorized in any explicit way, which gives a kind of 'superstructure' feel to the book, although frequent reference is given to the interrelationships with the 'base'. I will argue shortly that there is a wider sense in which theory is absent, not merely implicit in the analyses.

The eight chapters are relatively discrete essays, commonly discussing an elitist view of an aspect of Australian culture, then offering a counter-critique. This method underlines the general aim announced on the cover and in the Introduction, which is to 'extend our understanding of the Australian popular culture, and to counter the long-established, traditional criticism bewailing the lack of an Australian culture'. That an Australian culture does exist is unlikely to astonish students of cultural studies, which suggests that the book is partly aimed at engaging with the field of cultural criticism occupied by writers such as Donald Horne, Craig McGregor, Australian Ronald Conway and others, mentioned in the book.

More importantly, the 'traditional criticism' appears to take the role of dominant myths, while the critique offered by the authors is presumably a counter-myth, or even perhaps a new site of ideological struggle over such meanings. Unfortunately this is not made explicit and the short Introduction contains little theory of cultural dominance or competing discourses, let alone hegemony. In the absence of questions about myths that are dominant, the social bases of these, and of counter myths, one is left to suppose that the struggle is over who is right, who has objectivity on their side, rather than an account of competing myths and discourses, and the social interests and resources at stake. Nor is this just a matter of 'ideological soundness', but also a matter of theoretical and empirical adequacy which, in the end, is political because it continues or reinforces cultural myths and silences, rather than questioning and resisting them.

With these considerations in mind, questions that students of cultural studies should ask of a book on a culture's myths are: what are the myths explored; what is the thesis that the authors offer or assume about the myth; do the authors challenge the myth or reinforce it; is an objective account expressed or implied; what counter-myths are missing from the account? Using these questions as a framework, I will report briefly on three of the chapter areas that the authors analyse.

The first chapter examines the myth that Australian pubs are egalitarian, a view expressed by Craig McGregor,[1] who saw a 'no more classless place' (1967: 136). Subsidiary myths on alcohol and masculinity are also examined, beginning with a discussion of the 'birdwatchers bar' in Surfers Paradise.

Fiske et al. argue the following theses from their reading of these texts. Australian pubs are defined in relation to home (not-home), and to work (not-work). This involves semiotic analysis of the physical layout of pubs and their social relations, specifically family, gender, work, and mateship. Drinking and drunkenness can be seen to mean 'radical egalitarianism' in the context of wider social control and repressed feelings and aspirations, especially for working class, male drinkers. Alcohol as drink and drug gains its cultural meaning from the wider context of oppositions in consumer ideology, where beverages and narcotics from milk to meths and coke to cocaine are related together. Finally, pub rock is identified as the location of youth rebellion, where the Friday and Saturday night 'rage' combines the 'challenging, aggressive and violent' aspects of rock music, with alcoholic stimulants. This is a youthful version of 'Friday night out with the boys'.

It would be unfair to suggest that the authors do no more than repeat McGregor's view of the pub as the 'democratic leveller'. In fact they signal that McGregor would probably retreat from this claim himself. In relation to pub-rock they do use the language of dominant and oppositional myths, but see them as 'putative' and 'ideological'. However, in at least two of the readings they make of pubs (drunkenness and pub-rock), and especially in accepting the view that boss–worker relations are (almost) suspended when they drink together in pubs, there does appear significant sympathy with the myth of egalitarianism. There *are* myths in Australia that it is a classless society, and pubs might be cited as proof of this, and in the end Fiske *et al.* tend to reinforce this myth.

In their account of pubs, the authors do use objectivist language. In reading the traditional public bar they suggest that it is necessary to join neither 'the knockers' (cultural elitists) nor 'the drinkers'. This appears to privilege a position outside of those of the participants or their critics, and contradicts their claim in the introduction for a 'relativist' approach. What such a position might be, and how it is socially constructed or based, is not specified, but as Sless (1986)[2] has argued there can be no place outside social life from which to view any text. Given the constraints placed on readings by the wider culture and the specific context involved, the meaning of any text is not *in* the text but in the constructions that socially located observers give it.

It was suggested above that there are theoretically and politically important consequences for such objectivism, so what counter-myths are hidden by this analysis of Australian pubs? An important alternative view might be a feminist reading of the social meanings of pubs. Of course there is more than one feminism, but rather than offer a feminist analysis the aim is here to speculate on its concerns. The view of pubs as distinctively male domains would probably be a starting point for such an analysis, identifying it as a location for masculine values. This the authors do. Apart from the development of 'lounge bars, taverns and internationally-styled hotel bars' the traditional public bar 'retains its centrality and ubiquity'. In other words a feminist analysis could be built on insights found here but this is not the same as providing space for a woman-based counter-myth about pubs, as a hostile place for women to go. This claim might be qualified by recognition that even in the most traditional and sexist pubs there are places for women to go, such as the 'ladies' lounge', but this rather underlines the fact that women cannot go anywhere they choose in pubs.

Many women experience pubs as hostile, and a feminist analysis would probably claim that the decision of many women not to go to pubs, even in groups, is a 'correct reading' of the pub text. The absence of this point of view renders it invisible along with all the other silences in the representations of women's experience.

The fourth chapter 'Out of work' does deal with some counter-myths, discussing oppositional readings about work, unemployment, leisure (video games), TV quiz shows, and drama (as representations that relate to school and work). While no sign of the apparatus indicating 'dominant' and counter myths is displayed, this chapter does not appear to take 'traditional criticism' as a starting point. This may be why a dominant myth does not focus the discussion. However the authors do approach these texts from non-dominant trajectories. For example they analyse the experience of a young woman dealing with the Commonwealth Employment Scheme (which exhibits benign powerlessness toward her), the Job Centre (ambivalence) and the Department of Social Security (control and suspicion). Another example is the contradictory nature of the meanings of video games for people who use them, showing the way that young males wrest feelings of control from them. The point about these and other readings is that the dominant myths about the way that 'dole bludgers' and video games are perceived are effectively opposed. The chapter exposes some complexity and a strong sense of contradictory meanings.

The final chapter focuses on the Australian accent. The main myth here is that the success of the Australian accent in Australia (Paul Hogan was made 'Australian of the Year' in 1986), and overseas (with *Crocodile Dundee* and other films, Foster's Lager and Australian tourism), is gained at the loss of excellence and achievement. An example is analysed by the authors which connects the loss of excellence with the success of the current Labour prime minister, Bob Hawke. Here the accent is that of 'Hawkespeak'.

Fiske *et al.* focus on the way accents work, with some linguistic and historical background, as well as indicating some of the ways that the Aussie accent has been dealt with, in literature, film, comedy, the law, and TV. Taking the notion of accent further, to embrace wider aspects of the specific inflection of Australianness, the authors examine vegemite, thongs, and Australian Rules Football. Finally they turn to one of the more enduring myths, the elitist view that Australia is the 'lucky country', that the people are lazy and do not deserve or appreciate their good fortune.

In their desire to show the novel, enterprising, and creative dimensions of the Anglo-Australian cultural accent, the authors end up reinforcing, again by omission, a different kind of hegemonic myth. What the focus on Hogan and Hawke conceals is the linguistic and cultural 'accents' which are the sound and experience of Aboriginal and migrant Australians. The work of some researchers (e.g. Eades 1982)[3] has gone toward showing the particular linguistic form that constitutes 'Aboriginal English' as a language belonging to Aboriginal people. The particular combinations of Australian English with the inheritance of speaking either another variety of English (e.g. British migrants) or another language altogether, produces a specific range of Australian migrant accents that persist into the second or third generation at least, and are accompanied by wider cultural accents (often the basis of 'cross-cultural encounters', see Pride, 1985).[4]

A dominant representation of Australia and Australians always omits Aboriginal people (who are examined in the book in a number of contexts) and migrants (who are not discussed). Such omissions contribute to representations that are racist and xenophobic, reinforcing a widespread view suggesting that to be an Aboriginal or a migrant in Australia is to be, crucially, un-Australian (just as to be 'Asian' or West Indian in Britain is to be un-British). Any thought that this is not a live issue should be disproved by the current furore in Australia on 'multiculturalism'.

The invisibility of the difference of Aboriginal and migrant culture from the dominant Anglo culture is derived from both the starting point of this book (the concern for a lack of culture), and the objectivist theoretical position frequently taken by the authors. Without a theory of the social basis of any myth, the people and the culture are both hypostatized and homogenized. Without being able to offer a view of the nature of different myths in hierarchical cultures, whether preferred, negotiated, oppositional (Hall, 1973),[5] or hegemonic (Johnson, 1979; Bennett, 1986),[6] it is perhaps a matter of luck as to whether the readings that are generated cover the interests or representations of subordinate groups.

The unexamined objectivism that emerges in the vacuum of absent theory leads the authors in this case to reinvent some dominant myths, conceal the experience of whole social groups, and perpetuate representations that go to shape the consciousness of us all. This serves to legitimate dominant images, myth and ways of perceiving Australian culture.

In conclusion, the application of a semiotic approach to Australian popular culture is a relatively new enterprise, and the varied analyses in this book will broaden its appeal. But students of cultural studies and politics must avoid the attempt to deduce a single reading, and a single uncontested Australia from the texts.

Darling Downs Institute of Advanced Education,
Queensland, Australia

Notes

1 McGregor, C., *Profile of Australia*, Melbourne, Penguin, 1967.
2 Sless, D., *In Search of Semiotics*, New York, Barnes & Noble, 1986.
3 Eades, D., 'You gotta know how to talk . . .': ethnography of information-seeking in southeast Queensland Aboriginal society', *Australian Journal of Linguistics*, 2 (1): 61–82 (reprinted in Pride 1985), 1982.
4 Pride, J. (ed.) *Cross Cultural Encounters*, Rive: Seine, 1985.
5 Hall, S., 'The determinations of news photographs', in S. Cohen and J. Young (eds), *The Manufacture of News*, London, Constable, 1973.
6 Johnson, R., 'Histories of culture/theories of ideology: notes on an impasse', in M. Barrett *et al.* (eds), *Ideology and Cultural Production*, New York, St Martin's Press, 1979. See also Bennett, T., 'Popular culture and "the turn to Gramsci"', in Bennett *et al.* (eds), *Popular Culture and Social Relations*, Milton Keynes, Open University Press, 1986.

Printed in the United States
by Baker & Taylor Publisher Services